LEADERSHIP
and
MOTIVATION

Essays of Douglas McGregor

"The ingenuity and the perseverance of industrial management in the pursuit of economic ends have changed many scientific and technological dreams into commonplace realities. It is now becoming clear that the application of these same talents to the human side of enterprise will not only enhance substantially these materialistic achievements but will bring us one step closer to the 'good society.' Shall we get on with the job?"

Douglas McGregor
April 1957

LEADERSHIP
and
MOTIVATION

Essays of Douglas McGregor

Edited by Warren G. Bennis and Edgar H. Schein,
with the collaboration of Caroline McGregor

THE M.I.T. PRESS

Massachusetts Institute of Technology
Cambridge, Massachusetts, and London, England

Second printing, First M.I.T. Press paperback printing, February 1968
Third printing, April 1970
Fourth printing, March 1972
Fifth printing, July 1974

ISBN 0 262 13023 8 (hardcover)
ISBN 0 262 63015 X (paperback)

Library of Congress catalog card number 66-19362
Printed in the United States of America

To Doug's Friends

Contents

PART THREE

UNION-MANAGEMENT RELATIONS

PART FOUR

GROWTH AND DEVELOPMENT OF INDIVIDUALS AND GROUPS

PART FIVE

THE MANAGER AND THE HUMAN SCIENCES

Introduction

NOT UNTIL I BEGAN the task of introducing this book did
I get close to the themes of Doug McGregor's life and
how they shaped and informed his work. He was always so
immediate and spontaneous—as if only the present counted,
like a frontiersman—that though I knew he had a "past," so
to speak, I had not fully reckoned with its power. Caroline
McGregor helped me to understand this by providing judi-
cious fragments from Doug's family background and early
experiences and by other hints which I have only recently
been able to comprehend.

I confess that I am still too close to the man and to my
experiences with him to see him clearly, and I shall certainly
be unable to separate Doug's achievement from his life. Yet
his achievement was, to such a great extent, a basic encounter with life, and unthreading his personal experience from
his work would not only mislead but mutilate.

Doug drew his intellectual courage and maturity from the chronic tensions between powerful adversaries, internal and external, and he participated in this contest as staunch combatant and wise observer. His energy must surely have sprung from these encounters which he took as "lovers quarrels": threatening and alarming but, more often than not, way stations to integration and growth. Doug's humanness was due not to his conflicts, but to his loving confrontation with them. His commitment to learn from them was as great as his desire to resolve them.

I really had no idea of how deep and important the roots of conflicts were until I learned how John Murray McGregor, Doug's great grandfather, set a standard for the McGregors as a Scotch Presbyterian minister, and that his son, Thomas, made a living for a while by selling pianos and organs around Ohio, taking livestock for payment, and selling the livestock too. Not content with this, Thomas raised money from businessmen in Toledo to start a mission for transient laborers, with concern for their salvation as well as providing shelter and food. His dream was to build homes for homeless men in each of the industrial cities around the Great Lakes. He died of pneumonia after digging a foundation for what later became the McGregor Institute in Detroit. Tracy McGregor, Thomas's oldest son (and Doug's uncle) continued his father's work and started many other philanthropies in the Detroit area and, in fact, helped Doug finance his graduate education.

It might be useful if I quoted at length some personal correspondence from Caroline McGregor connected with Doug's family and background:

Doug's father became Director of the McGregor Institute in 1915. Family life revolved around this work—a chapel service every evening as well as the feeding and housing of as many as 700 men who were low on the totem pole of human dignity. Dad conducted service, played the organ, and Doug sometimes accompanied him on the piano, and Mother, who had a lovely contralto voice, occasionally sang. Both Doug and his brother worked in the office and at the desk out of school hours. Many of the staff were rehabilitated homeless men. Mother often had groups of the men for social evenings at the house.

Dad held strong religious beliefs, was a zealous Bible scholar and a lay preacher in his own right. As I look back on my first contacts with Doug's family, I am impressed with the deep concern for mankind, which Doug shared, and an equally deep pessimism in respect to man's potential goodness and strength, which Doug continued to challenge in his work and writings. It is significant that he chose to work with leaders in our society rather than the failures.

Although religion had a stern quality, there was a rich enjoyment of music by the entire family. Doug studied piano and "picked up" a number of other instruments. He was a skilled accompanist and traveled one summer with an evangelist. This is perhaps where he learned to swing *Onward Christian Soldiers*. Later, at Oberlin he directed a church choir for extra income.

This kind of an "upbringing," using that word in its old-fashioned sense, puts into focus the dominant chords in Doug's intellectual origins: religion, the search for meaning, music, and the firmly embedded idea that through productive work man will find his salvation. But the means to this end—of man's self-actualization—were wide apart. In fact, Doug and his father were engaged in a poignant correspondence in which each tried to articulate his philosophy of life right up to the time of Doug's death. In these letters, one surely detects the essence of two theories, both strongly held and deeply believed, and each at a tangent to the other.

In these letters and throughout his life, the main themes

of Doug's work shine through: his concern with bridging theory and practice, his desire to be true to his beliefs, regardless of the consequences, his *care* for others, his near obsession to communicate clearly, just a step away from evangelism, his concern for the dilemma of preserving autonomy within organized settings, a concern which we see clearly in his determination to confront realities no matter how threatening or uncomfortable, not out of a wistful desire for surface harmony, tempting as that might be to his temperament, but to sharpen his vision.

It was no accident that Doug's central theoretical worry, the last few years, was the "management of conflict." There is no doubt in my mind that his intellectual contribution was based on his uncanny capacity to *use himself* so splendidly. The fallout from his management of (and learning from) his own conflicts have given us an enhanced and more realistic vision of man's potential.

Nowhere more than at Antioch, during his presidency, did his stubborn desire for learning from his own conflicts show more vividly. (Turn to his essay, "On Leadership" for one sharp example.) As one of his colleagues wrote about him: "One of the most impressive things about Doug, perhaps it cannot be put in a formal biographical sketch, was his ability to absorb punishment. He was a very warm human being, reasonably conscious of his own shortcomings, and he accepted them as he accepted others' . . . criticism of them."

And another wrote: "Above all he was a born experimenter, a born innovator. He refused to accept what was, or the traditional, uncritically. And it may be that his greatest and most permeating achievement was to create an atmosphere in which students as well as faculty were stimulated to question and challenge continually in an effort to create an educational program that had a relationship to the whole of the life of the individual."

"If there was anything he was trying to overcome or destroy," another Antioch College faculty member said, "it was the institutional habit of talking about the virtues of democracy while running affairs autocratically."

Doug was a *learning man*. This means that he was always open to experience, to feedback; apparently, he did not require the ordinary cuticles of protection. This appetite for feedback began early in his career because, shortly after starting his teaching career at Harvard in 1935, he asked one of his senior professors for some help and guidance on his teaching style. After several paragraphs of praise, the professor, Gordon Allport, wrote:

> The only possible points I can think of that you might still learn are (1) not to jingle coins and keys, (2) keeping hands out of pockets would automatically prevent this, (3) generally speaking, feet belong on the floor rather than the lecture desk (though I am aware of the charm of informality expecially in a personality like yours . . .), (4) the trouble you will have next year is to get a theoretical framework into which to put things. I haven't succeeded very well in 12 years with this most difficult task.

Doug never succeeded in keeping his feet off the desk (Antioch students' sensibilities were apparently offended by this, too) but conquered the coin jingling unless he became impatient with late-staying guests, at which time he sounded like a one-man bell-ringing team. He did, though, finally construct a "theoretical framework into which to put things." In 1960, he wrote the distinguished *Human Side of Enterprise*, his only book and the culmination of wracking hours of work and thought.

But I do not think it was Doug's words or any single one of his essays that explain his impact. Rather, I tend to agree with Mason Haire who wrote that, "A large segment of his professional field operated in an environment which he created. Much of the work that goes on now couldn't have happened if he had never been."

Doug was, in the finest sense of that awkward phrase, a "change agent," able to change an entire concept of organizational man and to replace it with a theory that stressed man's potentials, emphasized man's growth, and elevated man's role in industrial society. Perhaps we cannot yet explain his impact. Perhaps none of these fragments begins to account for his contribution, and it was really his zest for life, his exuberant and childlike joy in living that meant everything, like swinging *Onward Christian Soldiers*.

The organization of the essays speaks for itself. They are not tightly organized and various areas overlap. There is some redundancy in the essays, but Ed Schein and I thought that they would prove valuable in showing the continuities and growth in Doug's thought, and we hope the readers will concur in this matter. Doug's mature style seemed to reconnect and coexist with an unresolved remnant of the past. His work was always "in process," so to speak, which makes clear-cut, "bench-mark" ideas impossible. We tried to be selective in the essays, choosing some from various periods in his career: Industrial Relations days at M.I.T., Antioch College presidency days, and then his return as Sloan Professor to M.I.T.'s Sloan School of Management. Unfortunately, we did not include anything from Doug's Harvard University period when he worked on color saturation (an obvious choice for a man who was himself color blind) and the prediction of social events, a beautiful study on a theme that haunted him throughout his career.

In closing, some acknowledgments are in order. First of all, to Caroline, who showed at all stages of preparation not only courage, which I have come to expect from her, but a solid intellectual support which never failed to influence me. Patricia (Patti to her friends) Macpherson, who for years was Doug's dedicated secretary, supporter, and friend, lovingly prepared the bibliography. Richard Beckhard helped at every step of the way and provided the necessary moral support when it was needed. Professor Ishwar Dayal, from the Indian Institute of Management, Calcutta, helped us with some of the choices and was always sensitive to the concerns of Doug's international public. Professors John Sparks and Douglass V. Brown helped out in all stages of preparation—John (with the help of Paul and Norma Bixler, Everett Wilson, Irwin Inman, Albert Stewart, Jessie Treichler, and Morris Keeton) for the Antioch College years, and Doug Brown for the whole period. His special friendship with Doug McGregor helped all of us by providing the necessary heart and vigor to continue our work.

WARREN G. BENNIS

Cambridge, Massachusetts
December 11, 1965

DOUGLAS McGREGOR

Outline of Career

Born September 16, 1906, Detroit, Michigan

Attended Thirkell School and Northwestern High School, class of 1923

1923–1926   City College of Detroit (now Wayne University)

1926   Oberlin College

1926–1930   Buffalo Grey Auto Stations; district manager, Albany and Detroit, 1927–1930

1928   Marriage to Caroline Ferris in Poughquag, New York

1930   Birth of daughter, Patricia Jane, in Detroit

1930–1932   With McGregor Institute, Detroit (transient laborers' shelter)

1931–1932   City College, Detroit; A.B., 1932

1932–1935   Graduate work in psychology, Harvard University; Ph.D., 1935

1935–1937   Instructor in Social Psychology, Harvard University

1937–1948   Instructor, Assistant Professor, Associate Professor, Professor of Psychology, Massachusetts Institute of Technology

1940   Birth of son, Peter Murray, in Arlington, Massachusetts

1943–1948   Executive Director of Industrial Relations Section, M.I.T.

1948–1954   President of Antioch College, Yellow Springs, Ohio

1954–1964   Professor of Industrial Management, M.I.T.; Sloan Fellows Professor, 1962–1964

1957–1960   Member of Nominating Committee for Faculty, M.I.T.

1960–1964   Member of Discipline Committee, M.I.T.; Chairman, 1962–1964

1961   Visiting Lecturer at Summer Advanced Management Program, Kashmir, India

1962   Member of Ad hoc Committee on Faculty Responsibility, M.I.T.

1963–1964   Chairman of Board of Governors of Endicott House

1964   Visiting Lecturer at Winter Advanced Management Program, sponsored by Indian Institute of Management, Calcutta, India

Consulting Relationships

1940–1948   Dewey and Almy Chemical Company; Director of Industrial Relations, 1943–1945

1945   U.S. Manpower Commission

1952–1963   Standard Oil Company of New Jersey and affiliates in Cuba, South America, and Saudi Arabia

1958–1960   The Champion Paper and Fibre Company

1961–1964   Bell Telephone Company of Pennsylvania

1963–1964   Union Carbide Corporation

1964   Imperial Chemical Industries, Ltd., Great Britain

Honors and Professional Societies

1949   Doctor of Laws, Wayne University

1952–1959   Member of Board, Social Science Research Council

1952–1954   Member of Board of Directors, Psychological Corporation

1954–1964   Member of Board, Foundation for Research in Human Behavior

1956   Phi Beta Kappa, Wayne University

1960–1963   Trustee of Antioch College, elected by alumni

1960–1964   Member of Visiting Committee to Harvard Psychology Department

1962   Sigma Iota Epsilon, Wayne University

1962   James A. Hamilton Hospital Administrators Book Award

Member, American Psychological Association, National Training Laboratories for Group Development, American Academy of Arts and Sciences, Sigma Xi

M.I.T. Faculty Resolution

The following resolution was formally presented to the assembled M.I.T. Faculty on October 21, 1964.

The Faculty records with deep regret the death of Douglas McGregor on October 13th, 1964. At the same time, it records with deep pride the contributions he made to M.I.T., to higher education throughout the United States, to the advancement of his chosen profession, to industry both here and abroad, and, above all, to the development of a great many individuals.

It is easy to relate the simple facts of his life. He was born in Detroit in 1906. He received his Bachelor's degree from Wayne University in 1932, his Master's degree from Harvard in 1933, and his Doctorate from Harvard in 1935. He came to M.I.T. in 1937, as one of the founders of the Industrial Relations Section. In 1948, when he was Professor of Psychology and Executive Director of the Industrial Relations Section, he accepted the position of President of Antioch College. After six years in this post, he returned to M.I.T. as Professor of Industrial Management, and in 1962 became the first incumbent of the Sloan Fellows Professorship. Along the way, he had served in many diverse capacities, among others as Director of Industrial Relations for the Dewey and Almy Chemical Company, as a Trustee of Antioch College, as a Director of the Social Science Research Council, as a Director of the National Training Laboratories, as a Director of the Psychological Corporation, as Chairman of our own Discipline Committee, and as a consultant to government and industry.

It is less easy to describe in brief compass the many facets of the man that Douglas McGregor was. He was a man of wide interests, from music to gardening, from company reorganization to the sharing of jokes, from education in India to the life of his family. To none of these interests was he content to play the role of mere spectator; always he was an active participant.

In the very best sense of the term, Douglas McGregor was a crusader. He believed in the work he was doing, and he believed that others could benefit by what he had to offer. He took himself seriously; otherwise he could not have accomplished what he did. But he never took himself too seriously, and therein lay much of the basis of his effectiveness. Because he understood himself and his own foibles, he was able to appreciate and sympathize with the foibles of others. His sense of humor was robust, but it never manifested itself in ridicule.

His professional contributions were of the highest order. As one of his colleagues has said: "A large segment of his professional field operated in an environment which he created. Much of the work that goes on now couldn't have happened if he had never been."

Through his writings, particularly *The Human Side of Enterprise*, and through personal contacts, he was known throughout the world. Although he traveled widely, it was impossible for him to meet all or even most of the demands to serve as teacher, speaker, consultant, or counselor. To his office came a constant stream of people from all parts of the globe. For all of them, it was a rewarding experience.

Douglas McGregor led a full life. Not the least of the measures of its fullness was the enrichment he gave to the lives of countless others.

> Benson R. Snyder
> Charles A. Myers
> Donald G. Marquis
> Howard W. Johnson
> Warren G. Bennis
> Douglass V. Brown, Chairman

October 21st, 1964

PART ONE

■

MANAGERIAL
PHILOSOPHY

I

—————

The Human Side of Enterprise

I T HAS BECOME TRITE to say that the most significant developments of the next quarter century will take place not in the physical but in the social sciences, that industry—the economic organ of society—has the fundamental know-how to utilize physical science and technology for the material benefit of mankind, and that we must now learn how to utilize the social sciences to make our human organizations truly effective.

Many people agree in principle with such statements; but so far they represent a pious hope—and little else. Consider with me, if you will, something of what may be involved when we attempt to transform the hope into reality.

—————

First published in *Adventure in Thought and Action,* Proceedings of the Fifth Anniversary Convocation of the School of Industrial Management, Massachusetts Institute of Technology, Cambridge, April 9, 1957. Cambridge, Mass.: M.I.T. School of Industrial Management, 1957; and reprinted in *The Management Review,* 1957, *46,* No. 11, 22–28.

I

Let me begin with an analogy. A quarter century ago basic conceptions of the nature of matter and energy had changed profoundly from what they had been since Newton's time. The physical scientists were persuaded that under proper conditions new and hitherto unimagined sources of energy could be made available to mankind.

We know what has happened since then. First came the bomb. Then, during the past decade, have come many other attempts to exploit these scientific discoveries—some successful, some not.

The point of my analogy, however, is that the application of theory in this field is a slow and costly matter. We expect it always to be thus. No one is impatient with the scientist because he cannot tell industry how to build a simple, cheap, all-purpose source of atomic energy today. That it will take at least another decade and the investment of billions of dollars to achieve results which are economically competitive with present sources of power is understood and accepted.

It is transparently pretentious to suggest any *direct* similarity between the developments in the physical sciences leading to the harnessing of atomic energy and potential developments in the social sciences. Nevertheless, the analogy is not as absurd as it might appear to be at first glance.

To a lesser degree, and in a much more tentative fashion, we are in a position in the social sciences today like that of the physical sciences with respect to atomic energy in the thirties. We know that past conceptions of the nature of man are inadequate and in many ways incorrect. We are becoming quite certain that, under proper conditions, unimagined resources of creative human energy could become available within the organizational setting.

We cannot tell industrial management how to apply this new knowledge in simple, economic ways. We know it will require years of exploration, much costly development research, and a substantial amount of creative imagination on the part of management to discover how to apply this growing knowledge to the organization of human effort in industry.

May I ask that you keep this analogy in mind—overdrawn and pretentious though it may be—as a framework for what I have to say this morning.

Management's Task: Conventional View

The conventional conception of management's task in harnessing human energy to organizational requirements can be stated broadly in terms of three propositions. In order to avoid the complications introduced by a label, I shall call this set of propositions "Theory X":

1. Management is responsible for organizing the elements of productive enterprise—money, materials, equipment, people—in the interest of economic ends.
2. With respect to people, this is a process of directing their efforts, motivating them, controlling their actions, modifying their behavior to fit the needs of the organization.
3. Without this active intervention by management, people would be passive—even resistant—to organizational needs. They must therefore be persuaded, rewarded, punished, controlled—their activities must be directed. This is management's task—in managing subordinate managers or workers. We often sum it up by saying that management consists of getting things done through other people.

Behind this conventional theory there are several additional beliefs—less explicit, but widespread:

4. The average man is by nature indolent—he works as little as possible.
5. He lacks ambition, dislikes responsibility, prefers to be led.
6. He is inherently self-centered, indifferent to organizational needs.
7. He is by nature resistant to change.
8. He is gullible, not very bright, the ready dupe of the charlatan and the demagogue.

The human side of economic enterprise today is fashioned from propositions and beliefs such as these. Conventional organization structures, managerial policies, practices, and programs reflect these assumptions.

In accomplishing its task—with these assumptions as guides —management has conceived of a range of possibilities between two extremes.

The Hard or the Soft Approach?

At one extreme, management can be "hard" or "strong." The methods for directing behavior involve coercion and threat (usually disguised), close supervision, tight controls over behavior. At the other extreme, management can be "soft" or "weak." The methods for directing behavior involve being permissive, satisfying people's demands, achieving harmony. Then they will be tractable, accept direction.

This range has been fairly completely explored during the past half century, and management has learned some things from the exploration. There are difficulties in the "hard" approach. Force breeds counterforces: restriction of output, antagonism, militant unionism, subtle but effective sabotage of management objectives. This approach is especially difficult during times of full employment.

There are also difficulties in the "soft" approach. It leads frequently to the abdication of management—to harmony, perhaps, but to indifferent performance. People take advantage of the soft approach. They continually expect more, but they give less and less.

Currently, the popular theme is "firm but fair." This is an attempt to gain the advantages of both the hard and the soft approaches. It is reminiscent of Teddy Roosevelt's "speak softly and carry a big stick."

Is the Conventional View Correct?

The findings which are beginning to emerge from the social sciences challenge this whole set of beliefs about man and human nature and about the task of management. The evidence is far from conclusive, certainly, but it is suggestive. It comes from the laboratory, the clinic, the schoolroom, the home, and even to a limited extent from industry itself.

The social scientist does not deny that human behavior in industrial organization today is approximately what management perceives it to be. He has, in fact, observed it and studied it fairly extensively. But he is pretty sure that this behavior is *not* a consequence of man's inherent nature. It is a consequence rather of the nature of industrial organizations, of management philosophy, policy, and practice. The conventional approach of Theory X is based on mistaken notions of what is cause and what is effect.

"Well," you ask, "what then is the *true* nature of man? What evidence leads the social scientist to deny what is obvious?" And, if I am not mistaken, you are also thinking, "Tell me—simply, and without a lot of scientific verbiage— what you think you know that is so unusual. Give me—

without a lot of intellectual claptrap and theoretical non-sense—some practical ideas which will enable me to improve the situation in my organization. And remember, I'm faced with increasing costs and narrowing profit margins. I want proof that such ideas won't result simply in new and costly human relations frills. I want practical results, and I want them now."

If these are your wishes, you are going to be disappointed. Such requests can no more be met by the social scientist to-day than could comparable ones with respect to atomic energy be met by the physicist fifteen years ago. I can, how-ever, indicate a few of the reasons for asserting that conven-tional assumptions about the human side of enterprise are inadequate. And I can suggest—tentatively—some of the propositions that will compose a more adequate theory of the management of people. The magnitude of the task that confronts us will then, I think, be apparent.

II

Perhaps the best way to indicate why the conventional approach of management is inadequate is to consider the sub-ject of motivation. In discussing this subject I will draw heavily on the work of my colleague, Abraham Maslow of Brandeis University. His is the most fruitful approach I know. Naturally, what I have to say will be overgeneralized and will ignore important qualifications. In the time at our disposal, this is inevitable.

Physiological and Safety Needs

Man is a wanting animal—as soon as one of his needs is satisfied, another appears in its place. This process is unend-ing. It continues from birth to death.

Man's needs are organized in a series of levels—a hierarchy of importance. At the lowest level, but preeminent in importance when they are thwarted, are his physiological needs. Man lives by bread alone, when there is no bread. Unless the circumstances are unusual, his needs for love, for status, for recognition are inoperative when his stomach has been empty for a while. But when he eats regularly and adequately, hunger ceases to be an important need. The sated man has hunger only in the sense that a full bottle has emptiness. The same is true of the other physiological needs of man—for rest, exercise, shelter, protection from the elements.

A satisfied need is not a motivator of behavior! This is a fact of profound significance. It is a fact that is regularly ignored in the conventional approach to the management of people. I shall return to it later. For the moment, one example will make my point. Consider your own need for air. Except as you are deprived of it, it has no appreciable motivating effect upon your behavior.

When the physiological needs are reasonably satisfied, needs at the next higher level begin to dominate man's behavior—to motivate him. These are called safety needs. They are needs for protection against danger, threat, deprivation. Some people mistakenly refer to these as needs for security. However, unless man is in a dependent relationship where he fears arbitrary deprivation, he does not demand security. The need is for the "fairest possible break." When he is confident of this, he is more than willing to take risks. But when he feels threatened or dependent, his greatest need is for guarantees, for protection, for security.

The fact needs little emphasis that, since every industrial employee is in a dependent relationship, safety needs may assume considerable importance. Arbitrary management actions, behavior that arouses uncertainty with respect to continued employment or which reflects favoritism or discrimination, unpredictable administration of policy—these can be powerful motivators of the safety needs in the employment relationship *at every level* from worker to vice president.

Social Needs

When man's physiological needs are satisfied and he is no longer fearful about his physical welfare, his social needs become important motivators of his behavior—for belonging, for association, for acceptance by his fellows, for giving and receiving friendship and love.

Management knows today of the existence of these needs, but it often assumes quite wrongly that they represent a threat to the organization. Many studies have demonstrated that the tightly knit, cohesive work group may, under proper conditions, be far more effective than an equal number of separate individuals in achieving organizational goals.

Yet management, fearing group hostility to its own objectives, often goes to considerable lengths to control and direct human efforts in ways that are inimical to the natural "groupiness" of human beings. When man's social needs—and perhaps his safety needs, too—are thus thwarted, he behaves in ways which tend to defeat organizational objectives. He becomes resistant, antagonistic, uncooperative. But this behavior is a consequence, not a cause.

Ego Needs

Above the social needs—in the sense that they do not become motivators until lower needs are reasonably satisfied—are the needs of greatest significance to management and to man himself. They are the egoistic needs, and they are of two kinds:

1. Those needs that relate to one's self-esteem—needs for self-confidence, for independence, for achievement, for competence, for knowledge.
2. Those needs that relate to one's reputation—needs for status, for recognition, for appreciation, for the deserved respect of one's fellows.

Unlike the lower needs, these are rarely satisfied; man seeks indefinitely for more satisfaction of these needs once they have become important to him. But they do not appear in any significant way until physiological, safety, and social needs are all reasonably satisfied.

The typical industrial organization offers few opportunities for the satisfaction of these egoistic needs to people at lower levels in the hierarchy. The conventional methods of organizing work, particularly in mass-production industries, give little heed to these aspects of human motivation. If the practices of scientific management were deliberately calculated to thwart these needs—which, of course, they are not—they could hardly accomplish this purpose better than they do.

Self-Fulfillment Needs

Finally—a capstone, as it were, on the hierarchy of man's needs—there are what we may call the needs for self-fulfillment. These are the needs for realizing one's own potentialities, for continued self-development, for being creative in the broadest sense of that term.

It is clear that the conditions of modern life give only limited opportunity for these relatively weak needs to obtain expression. The deprivation most people experience with respect to other lower-level needs diverts their energies into the struggle to satisfy *those* needs, and the needs for self-fulfillment remain dormant.

III

Now, briefly, a few general comments about motivation:

We recognize readily enough that a man suffering from a severe dietary deficiency is sick. The deprivation of physiological needs has behavioral consequences. The same is true—although less well recognized—of deprivation of higher-level needs. The man whose needs for safety, association, independence, or status are thwarted is sick just as surely as is he who has rickets. And his sickness will have behavioral consequences. We will be mistaken if we attribute his resultant passivity, his hostility, his refusal to accept responsibility to his inherent "human nature." These forms of behavior are *symptoms* of illness—of deprivation of his social and egoistic needs.

The man whose lower-level needs are satisfied is not motivated to satisfy those needs any longer. For practical purposes they exist no longer. (Remember my point about your need for air.) Management often asks, "Why aren't people more productive? We pay good wages, provide good working conditions, have excellent fringe benefits and steady employment. Yet people do not seem to be willing to put forth more than minimum effort."

The fact that management has provided for these physiological and safety needs has shifted the motivational emphasis to the social and perhaps to the egoistic needs. Unless there are opportunities *at work* to satisfy these higher-level needs, people will be deprived; and their behavior will reflect this deprivation. Under such conditions, if management continues to focus its attention on physiological needs, its efforts are bound to be ineffective.

People *will* make insistent demands for more money under these conditions. It becomes more important than ever to buy the material goods and services that can provide limited satisfaction of the thwarted needs. Although money has only limited value in satisfying many higher-level needs, it can become the focus of interest if it is the *only* means available.

The Carrot and Stick Approach

The carrot and stick theory of motivation (like Newtonian physical theory) works reasonably well under certain circumstances. The *means* for satisfying man's physiological and (within limits) his safety needs can be provided or withheld by management. Employment itself is such a means, and so are wages, working conditions, and benefits. By these means the individual can be controlled so long as he is struggling for subsistence. Man lives for bread alone when there is no bread.

But the carrot and stick theory does not work at all once man has reached an adequate subsistence level and is motivated primarily by higher needs. Management cannot provide a man with self-respect, or with the respect of his fellows, or with the satisfaction of needs for self-fulfillment. It can create conditions such that he is encouraged and enabled to seek such satisfactions *for himself*, or it can thwart him by failing to create those conditions.

But this creation of conditions is not "control." It is not a good device for directing behavior. And so management finds itself in an odd position. The high standard of living created by our modern technological know-how provides quite adequately for the satisfaction of physiological and safety needs. The only significant exception is where management practices have not created confidence in a "fair break"—and thus where safety needs are thwarted. But by making possible the satisfaction of low-level needs, management has deprived itself of the ability to use as motivators the devices on which conventional theory has taught it to rely—rewards, promises, incentives, or threats and other coercive devices.

Neither Hard Nor Soft

The philosophy of management by direction and control —*regardless of whether it is hard or soft*—is inadequate to motivate, because the human needs on which this approach relies are today unimportant motivators of behavior. Direction and control are essentially useless in motivating people whose important needs are social and egoistic. Both the hard and the soft approach fail today because they are simply irrelevant to the situation.

People deprived of opportunities to satisfy at work the needs that are now important to them behave exactly as we might predict—with indolence, passivity, resistance to change, lack of responsibility, willingness to follow the demagogue, unreasonable demands for economic benefits. It would seem that we are caught in a web of our own weaving.

In summary, then, of these comments about motivation:

Management by direction and control—whether implemented with the hard, the soft, or the firm but fair approach —fails under today's conditions to provide effective motivation of human effort toward organizational objectives. It fails because direction and control are useless methods of motivating people whose physiological and safety needs are reasonably satisfied and whose social, egoistic, and self-fulfillment needs are predominant.

IV

For these and many other reasons, we require a different theory of the task of managing people based on more adequate assumptions about human nature and human motivation. I am going to be so bold as to suggest the broad dimensions of such a theory. Call it "Theory Y," if you will.

1. Management is responsible for organizing the elements of productive enterprise—money, materials, equipment, people—in the interest of economic ends.
2. People are *not* by nature passive or resistant to organizational needs. They have become so as a result of experience in organizations.
3. The motivation, the potential for development, the capacity for assuming responsibility, the readiness to direct behavior toward organizational goals are all present in people. Management does not put them there. It is a responsibility of management to make it possible for people to recognize and develop these human characteristics for themselves.
4. The essential task of management is to arrange organizational conditions and methods of operation so that people can achieve their own goals *best* by directing *their own* efforts toward organizational objectives.

This is a process primarily of creating opportunities, releasing potential, removing obstacles, encouraging growth, providing guidance. It is what Peter Drucker has called "management by objectives" in contrast to "management by control."

And I hasten to add that it does *not* involve the abdication of management, the absence of leadership, the lowering of standards, or the other characteristics usually associated with the "soft" approach under Theory X. Much on the contrary. It is no more possible to create an organization today which will be a fully effective application of this theory than it was to build an atomic power plant in 1945. There are many formidable obstacles to overcome.

Some Difficulties

The conditions imposed by conventional organization theory and by the approach of scientific management for the past half century have tied men to limited jobs which do not utilize their capabilities, have discouraged the acceptance of responsibility, have encouraged passivity, have eliminated meaning from work. Man's habits, attitudes, expectations— his whole conception of membership in an industrial organization—have been conditioned by his experience under these circumstances. Change in the direction of Theory Y will be slow, and it will require extensive modification of the attitudes of management and workers alike.

People today are accustomed to being directed, manipulated, controlled in industrial organizations and to finding satisfaction for their social, egoistic, and self-fulfillment needs away from the job. This is true of much of management as well as of workers. Genuine "industrial citizenship" —to borrow again a term from Drucker—is a remote and unrealistic idea, the meaning of which has not even been considered by most members of industrial organizations.

Another way of saying this is that Theory X places exclusive reliance upon external control of human behavior, whereas Theory Y relies heavily on self-control and self-direction. It is worth noting that this difference is the difference between treating people as children and treating them as mature adults. After generations of the former, we cannot expect to shift to the latter overnight.

V

Before we are overwhelmed by the obstacles, let us remember that the application of theory is always slow. Progress is usually achieved in small steps.

Consider with me a few innovative ideas which are entirely consistent with Theory Y and which are today being applied with some success.

Decentralization and Delegation

These are ways of freeing people from the too-close control of conventional organization, giving them a degree of freedom to direct their own activities, to assume responsibility, and, importantly, to satisfy their egoistic needs. In this connection, the flat organization of Sears, Roebuck and Company provides an interesting example. It forces "management by objectives" since it enlarges the number of people reporting to a manager until he cannot direct and control them in the conventional manner.

Job Enlargement

This concept, pioneered by I.B.M. and Detroit Edison, is quite consistent with Theory Y. It encourages the acceptance of responsibility at the bottom of the organization; it s opportunities for satisfying social and egoistic In fact, the reorganization of work at the factory ffers one of the more challenging opportunities for innovation consistent with Theory Y. The studies by A. T. M. Wilson and his associates of British coal mining and Indian textile manufacture have added appreciably to our understanding of work organization. Moreover, the economic and psychological results achieved by this work have been substantial.

Participation and Consultative Management

Under proper conditions these results provide encouragement to people to direct their creative energies toward organizational objectives, give them some voice in decisions that affect them, provide significant opportunities for the satisfaction of social and egoistic needs. I need only mention the Scanlon Plan as the outstanding embodiment of these ideas in practice.

The not infrequent failure of such ideas as these to work as well as expected is often attributable to the fact that a management has "bought the idea" but applied it within the framework of Theory X and its assumptions.

Delegation is not an effective way of exercising management by control. Participation becomes a farce when it is applied as a sales gimmick or a device for kidding people into thinking they are important. Only the management that has confidence in human capacities and is itself directed toward organizational objectives rather than toward the preservation of personal power can grasp the implications of this emerging theory. Such management will find and apply successfully other innovative ideas as we move slowly toward the full implementation of a theory like Y.

Performance Appraisal

Before I stop, let me mention one other practical application of Theory Y which—though still highly tentative—may well have important consequences. This has to do with performance appraisal within the ranks of management. Even a cursory examination of conventional programs of performance appraisal will reveal how completely consistent they are with Theory X. In fact, most such programs tend to treat the individual as though he were a product under inspection on the assembly line.

Take the typical plan: substitute "product" for "subordinate being appraised," substitute "inspector" for "superior making the appraisal," substitute "rework" for "training or development," and, except for the attributes being judged, the human appraisal process will be virtually indistinguishable from the product-inspection process.

A few companies—among them General Mills, Ansul Chemical, and General Electric—have been experimenting with approaches which involve the individual in setting "targets" or objectives *for himself* and in a *self*-evaluation of performance semiannually or annually. Of course, the superior plays an important leadership role in this process—one, in fact, that demands substantially more competence than the conventional approach. The role is, however, considerably more congenial to many managers than the role of "judge" or "inspector" which is forced upon them by conventional performance. Above all, the individual is encouraged to take a greater responsibility for planning and appraising his own contribution to organizational objectives; and the accompanying effects on egoistic and self-fulfillment needs are substantial. This approach to performance appraisal represents one more innovative idea being explored by a few managements who are moving toward the implementation of Theory Y.

VI

And now I am back where I began. I share the belief that we could realize substantial improvements in the effectiveness of industrial organizations during the next decade or two. Moreover, I believe the social sciences can contribute much to such developments. We are only beginning to grasp the implications of the growing body of knowledge in these fields. But if this conviction is to become a reality instead of a pious hope, we will need to view the process much as we view the process of releasing the energy of the atom for constructive human ends—as a slow, costly, sometimes discouraging approach toward a goal which would seem to many to be quite unrealistic.

The ingenuity and the perseverance of industrial management in the pursuit of economic ends have changed many scientific and technological dreams into commonplace realities. It is now becoming clear that the application of these same talents to the human side of enterprise will not only enhance substantially these materialistic achievements but will bring us one step closer to "the good society." Shall we get on with the job?

2

New Concepts of Management

I SHARE with a number of colleagues in the field of management, and with a few managers, the conviction that we will witness during the next couple of decades some profound, far-reaching changes in the strategy utilized to manage the human resources of enterprise. These changes will not be superficial modifications in current practice, but basic revisions of certain concepts that have dominated management thinking during the past half century or more.

The circumstances that will ultimately force these changes are already developing, but their significance is not yet widely recognized. They can be summed up in terms of four trends that are clearly apparent in our society today:

(1) *The explosive growth of science* (both behavioral and physical), which is yielding knowledge relevant to every function of enterprise—finance, sales, advertising,

Read at a conference on "Executive Responsibilities in a Period of Exploding Technology," which was held at M.I.T.; and published in *The Technology Review*, 1961, *63*, No. 4, 2–4.

public relations, personnel, purchasing, manufacturing—as well as research and engineering.

(2) *The rapidly increasing complexity of technology* in both office and factory—and in related aspects of everyday life such as transportation and communication.

(3) *The growing complexity of industry-society relationships* with government, consumers, suppliers, unions, stockholders, and the public generally. As a result of world-wide economic development, relations with other cultures will add substantially to these complexities.

(4) *The changing composition of the industrial work force.* Today more than half the employees of industry in the United States are white-collar. Within the white-collar group, we are witnessing a rapid growth of "exempt" salaried personnel, which includes managers and professionally trained people of all kinds. In one large company, the exempt salaried group has grown from 19 per cent to 35 per cent of total employment in the last decade. The curve is accelerating in line with Parkinson's law, but for reasons other than his witty analysis would suggest.

One major consequence of these trends is that in a few years the single largest and most influential class of employees in most industrial organizations will be professional managers and specialists of many kinds, populating every department and every function. Their utilization of various branches of scientific knowledge to solve practical problems will be the primary basis for planning, decision making, and policy formulation from top to bottom of the organization. As a result of the first three trends I have mentioned, they will be both indispensable and powerful, and the necessity to make full use of their competence and training will force a revolution in managerial strategy.

The conventional strategy of management—and the policies and practices as well as organization structures that have developed to serve it—was evolved with the blue-collar wage earner as its primary object. Even he is changing substantially in his education, economic status, attitudes, and competence. But the primary problems of the next several decades will center around the professional specialist. Our present strategy, policies, and practices are quite inappropriate to the task of directing and controlling his efforts. Briefly, let us see why.

Intellectual Creativity

The first and most important reason is the nature of the professional's contribution to the success of the enterprise. His work consists essentially of creative intellectual effort to aid management in its policy making, problem solving, planning, decision making, and administrative activities.

Such professional work cannot be "programmed" and directed the way we program and direct an assembly line or an accounting department. The methods of the industrial engineer are simply irrelevant to it. The management of such work consists chiefly in establishing objectives—the hoped-for results—and in obtaining the professional's commitment to them. It is part of the professional's unique value that he is capable of determining the steps necessary to achieve the desired objectives. Often he knows more about this than his boss does.

This kind of intellectual contribution to the enterprise cannot be obtained by giving orders, by traditional supervisory practices, or by close systems of control, such as we now apply to blue-collar and clerical workers. Even conventional notions of productivity—based as they are on concepts of effort per small unit of time such as the hour or day —are meaningless with reference to the creative intellectual effort of the professional specialist.

In addition, the complexity of the problems to be solved, the nature of the decisions to be made, frequently will demand collaborative effort by many professional specialists from *different* fields ranging clear across the behavioral, biological, and physical sciences. As yet, management has acquired but little knowledge or skill with respect to the management of such collaborative teams, or in developing organizational structures that will provide for their effective utilization.

There has been considerable interest in recent years in "creativity," but this interest has centered on identifying people with creative potential and on such gimmicks as brainstorming. Management has not yet considered in any depth what is involved in *managing* an organization heavily populated with people whose prime contribution consists of creative intellectual effort.

Professional specialists are human beings, of course, but their values, their expectations, and their needs are substantially different from those of the blue-collar worker on whom we have lavished our attention in the past.

What Professionals Want

Economic rewards are certainly important to the professional, but there is ample research to demonstrate that they do not provide the *primary* incentive to peak performance. Management's real task with respect to economic rewards is to administer them in ways that professional employees accept as *equitable*, in order to avoid dissatisfactions and pre-occupations that interfere with performance. If they are poorly administered, economic rewards can *lower* productivity below a modest, satisfactory level; they do not appear to be particularly potent in raising it above that level.

Much more crucial to the professional—*provided economic rewards are equitable*—are such things as:

Full utilization of his talent and training, which means critical attention to the nature of his work, the organization of the functions in which he participates, the challenge built into his job, and his freedom from close and detailed supervision.

His status, not only within the organization but externally with respect to his profession. Our tendency to regard staff functions, where most professionals reside, as "burdens" on production is but one way in which we prevent him from achieving status.

In addition, despite some rather paternalistic concessions such as permission to attend professional society meetings, management tends to bind the professional to the enterprise in a fashion that minimizes his opportunity to achieve status and recognition among his colleagues in his field. Publication, and participation in the affairs of professional societies are far more important sources of status than mere attendance at meetings. Yet, even where competitive secrets are not involved, such activities often are regarded as undesirable distractions from the professional's primary responsibilities to his company. In fact, they contribute to his value, as well as to his status and satisfaction.

His opportunities for development within his professional career. Our elaborate programs for *management* development provide few opportunities today for the *career* development of professional specialists.

Conventional policies and practices with respect to promotion penalize the man who does not aspire to a managerial job, by requiring him to change his function and assume different responsibilities. Promotion, for the professional, means receiving rewards and recognition for doing better exactly what he has been doing already. Management has given little heed to these values of the professional so far, or to their policy implications. The professional's long-term career expectations are of fundamental importance to him. In private practice or in academic institutions, he is accustomed to choosing among alternative opportunities in terms of these values. Industrial management, on the other hand, is accustomed to exercising a substantial amount of "career authority" over its managerial employees at all levels. The individual is evaluated, promoted, rotated, and transferred in terms of the needs of the organization almost irrespective of his personal career motivations. These incompatible points of view are certain to come into conflict as professional employees become more numerous and more indispensable to industry.

This inconsistency, it is worth noting, has political implications of more than minor significance. One of the distinguishing features of our Western democratic society, we proudly affirm, is that the individual is *not* the servant of the state. It is interesting that the largest and most powerful institution in this same Western society—industry—characteristically administers promotion policies (which profoundly affect the lifetime careers of its employees) with almost complete emphasis on "the needs of the organization." Only his freedom to quit—a freedom that is often too costly to exercise after he has built up a substantial equity in company benefit plans—protects the individual from being in fact "a servant of the corporation" in this rather basic way.

Two Qualifications

Among the qualifications that should be discussed, with respect to these generalizations, two must be mentioned to prevent misunderstanding.

First, I have talked about a class of people—professional specialists—as though they were all alike, all possessed of the same attitudes, expectations, values, and needs. Obviously, they are not; like any other class of human beings, they differ one from the other in every one of the respects I have mentioned.

Behavioral scientists have studied two groups of professionals lying at the extremes of a range. At one extreme are the "locals" who readily adjust their values and aspirations to the organization that employs them. At the other end are the "cosmopolitans" whose primary identification is with their professional field regardless of where they are employed. Note, however, that there is no evidence to indicate that competence, ability, or potential contribution to the organization are localized in any one part of this range. The comments I have made about professionals should be taken as applying broadly to the middle of the continuum.

Second, although I have directed your attention to a single class of employees, it is obvious that the trends in our society will affect other groups as well. Line managers, for example, will themselves inevitably become more professional, both in training and outlook. The work of wage earners and clerical personnel, as well as their attitudes and expectations, will be materially affected. The growth in numbers and influence of professional specialists in every function of the business will nevertheless be the most dramatic of these changes, and the one requiring the most drastic alterations in management strategy.

Self-Direction Is Essential

The four trends described earlier will necessitate many changes in traditional managerial policy and practice. None of them will come about easily, or by superficial modifications in conventional practice. Personnel "gadgetry" will not do the job.

Perhaps the primary change will be in a deep-seated and long-standing conception of managerial control. This conception concerns the necessity for imposing direction and limitations on the individual in order to get him to perform the work for which he is hired. It is, however, an observable characteristic of human beings that they will exercise *self*-direction and *self*-control in the service of objectives to which they are committed. These are matters of degree, of course, but I find few managements who are consciously moving in the direction of substituting self-control for externally imposed controls. The movement, if any, appears to be in the opposite direction, because this concept of self-control is erroneously associated with "soft" management.

In the recognition of this capacity of human beings to exercise self-control lies the only fruitful opportunity for industrial management to realize the full potential represented by professional resources. Creative intellectual effort of the kind upon which management will increasingly rely—in order to remain competitive—is a function of genuine commitment to objectives, under conditions that provide for a substantial degree of *self*-direction and *self*-control.

It is for this reason above all that I believe we are going to see a basic, almost revolutionary change in managerial strategy during the next two or three decades. It will not be possible in the future—because of the trends outlined earlier —for management to rely exclusively on intuition and past experience and "common sense," either in making or implementing its decisions. It will be no more possible tomorrow to manage an industrial enterprise than it is today to fly a jet aircraft "by the seat of the pants." Creative intellectual effort by a wide range of professional specialists will be as essential to tomorrow's manager as instruments and an elaborate air-traffic-control system are to today's jet pilot.

But traditional managerial strategy is primarily geared to the elaborately "programmed" and closely supervised activities of the blue-collar production worker and the clerical employee. As professional specialists become the single largest and most important class of employees in the enterprise, this traditional strategy will become hopelessly inadequate. Its greatest inadequacy will be with respect to its central concepts concerning the control of organized human effort. Management by objectives and self-control will inevitably replace management by authority and externally imposed control. In the long run this change in strategy will affect not only professional employees but all the human resources of enterprise.

Industrial management is not entirely unaware of the necessity for change in its strategy. There is already some genuine concern over the inadequacy of current methods of control. Symptoms of underlying difficulties have been apparent for some time in industrial research laboratories (where professionals are numerous) and in engineering functions (where they are becoming so). But there is as yet little recognition that these are symptoms that will soon spread to every phase of business activity. When this recognition does occur, we will have the impetus for the development of a new managerial strategy without which the enterprise of the future will be unable to prosper.

3

A Philosophy of Management

I HAVE THE IMPRESSION, as I wander around the industrial scene, that there is a considerable overemphasis today on the importance of "gadgets" in the field of human relations. A variety of devices, policies, formulas, methods, and techniques are used in the attempt to solve our problems of effective management, of effective human relations. Not only is it true in industry, where we seem to be pretty gadget-minded anyway, but there are even little books on how to bring up your children, how to improve your personality, or how to become a leader. Then there are methods like job evaluation, merit rating, supervisory training, and incentive wages which also frequently take on a gadget character.

I am not opposed to methods, techniques, and formulas, but I want to make a point about them: their value and usefulness depend on the attitudes and the points of view of the people who use them. There is always something that lies

A talk presented to the Management Forum of E. I. du Pont de Nemours Co. in 1954.

behind the method which is critically significant in determining whether the method works or not.

Management through Gadgets

In Dale Carnegie's book, *How to Win Friends and Influence People*, there are some nice formulas and some nice little gadgets to use in winning friends and influencing people. But suppose we have a man who fundamentally mistrusts people, and who believes that on the whole they are rather stupid. He believes that most of them cannot really be trusted and are not particularly friendly by nature. Suppose this man sets out to apply the principles, the gadgets, that Dale Carnegie outlines. Perhaps you will agree with me that such a man will not make these methods work; in fact they may boomerang because he will use them with his tongue in his cheek. He will use them with a manner that makes it immediately apparent that they are something superficial he has taken on, that they are tools he does not really believe in. He will not win friends and influence people. On the contrary, he is more likely to make enemies by following the principles of Dale Carnegie.

I sat in a meeting a few weeks ago with a group of office department heads in a small company in Cambridge. They were considering the problem of getting people to arrive on time in the morning. What interested me was the way the conversation went in that group. One man said the solution was to install time clocks. Someone else said to take a little book and put it in a prominent place on a desk at the front of each department and require anybody who came in after the starting hour of 8:30 to sign his name in the book and the hour of his arrival at work. Another man, a little more ingenious than the rest perhaps, suggested that in his department he could arrange a turnstile at the door to the office in such a way that anybody coming in after 8:30 would ring a bell which would be heard in the whole department.

These were serious suggestions made by a group of supervisors who in general are doing a good job. They thought of that problem entirely in terms of the gadgets they could use to solve it. What they did not think of were the attitudes and the backgrounds that they were bringing to bear on the problem.

I saw in that discussion inherent, although never expressed, feelings of this kind: "Coming to work on time is something that people won't do voluntarily."

That conviction was there, or they would not have been talking about gadgets to make people come to work on time. An additional feeling that never got expressed was, "This isn't our responsibility as supervisors. Let the gadgets do it; or let the Personnel Department do it." That they should be responsible for getting their people to work on time, in a personal sense, and for doing something about it if they continued to come late, somehow did not come out. It was below the surface and was never brought out into the open.

Those attitudes and convictions about people, those conceptions of the supervisor's job, were what was responsible for the suggestions they made for solving the problem. Those attitudes certainly would have determined the use that was made of their suggestions if any of them had been adopted. I will bet my shirt that not one of the suggestions considered at that meeting could be made to work as long as those attitudes were behind what the supervisors were talking about.

Today I want to talk chiefly about a "philosophy of management." In using that word I do not want to frighten you. My point is simply this: first of all, I believe that good leadership in industry depends more than any other single thing on the manager's conception of what his job is—of what management is. Second, it depends on his convictions and on his beliefs about people. Are people inherently honest; can they be taught to be honest? Will people naturally seek responsibility under certain conditions; or do you have to fight with them to get them to accept responsibility? Will people in general break rules no matter what the rules are; or is it possible that people will live up to rules voluntarily? Convictions about matters like these make up the philosophy that lies behind the manager's job. That is what I propose to talk about.

I am not going to try to impose my philosophy on you. However, I am going to talk about some things I believe to be true about people and about the manager's job. My purpose is to get you thinking about your own philosophy. Too often we take for granted our convictions and beliefs and attitudes relating to our job as managers. Too seldom do we get them out on the table and examine them and say, "Is this realistic? Is this the way people are? Is this what my job is?" My purpose is to get you to think about your philosophy by discussing mine with you.

Management by Force

First of all, it seems to me that the job of management can be defined pretty simply. It is to achieve the objective of the organization of which management is a part. I am talking now about all management from the very top to the very bottom. Management's job is to achieve the objective of the enterprise, and that purpose in our economy today may likewise be fairly simply stated: it is the production and sale of goods or services at a profit. That is what industrial enterprises exist for, and management is hired to accomplish that purpose.

The organization that management works with consists of plant, equipment, materials, machines, and people. To integrate all of those things, to organize them in such a way that the objective of the organization is achieved, is the job of management. In earlier days, management tended to treat plant, equipment, materials, and people without differentiating between them. We had what the economists now refer to as the "commodity theory of labor." This was the idea that the labor of people who worked for the enterprise could be bought and sold in the same way as the materials that were used. Various managements, small and large, treated people exactly that way. They did not differentiate between the machine and the person as far as managerial tactics were concerned.

Unfortunately, for management at any rate, it did not work too well. People were not docile, they were not as passive as the machinery in relation to management's wishes. If you get a machine properly set up, you push a button and the machine operates; it does not talk back to you or resist you.

Initially, in the early days after the Industrial Revolution, people were pretty docile. However, as the standard of living got a little higher, and people got a greater sense of dignity and personal responsibility, they began to get active themselves. Frequently, management found that the people were interfering with management's task of achieving the organizational objective through restriction of output or failure to live up to rules, by not doing what they were told, and sometimes through strikes and open rebellion of one kind or another. Some managements were faced with that kind of problem and for the first time had to differentiate between the material and human aspects of the organization.

Operating from the point of view that their job was to get the organization's purpose achieved through manipulating the ingredients, some managements simply said, "Well, if people won't be docile, we'll make them." The philosophy behind the tactics of such a management was, essentially, "Be strong, be tough, break down resistance and antagonism, and get the job done that way." The trick is to make people afraid through fear of unemployment. Even today, we find among some managements traces of that feeling. Some managers say, "I wish, fundamentally, that we could have a pretty severe depression again, because in a depression, when there are a lot more people than there are jobs, people do what they are told. They don't stand up on their hind legs and sneer at the boss. They are not insubordinate; they don't assert themselves the way they do when there is lots of work. It would be nice if we had a depression so we, management, could get in the driver's seat."

The difficulty with a philosophy of management that demands docile people and that argues, "if they are not docile we must make them become docile," is simply that it does not work, because it ignores a fundamental point that most of us know about human behavior. Psychologists dress this point up in fancy terms. They talk about the "frustration-aggression hypothesis." The idea is simply this: it is a primitive, natural, normal human reaction when we are frustrated —when we are blocked in attempting to achieve satisfaction of our needs—to kick back, to fight. You see it in the small child who, when reprimanded by papa, tends naturally to kick papa in the shins. Of course, the child learns quickly that this does not work. He discovers that it means more frustration. The child may revert to ways of expressing his aggression toward papa that are a little more subtle, but they accomplish the same purpose.

You come home some night tired and worn out. The things you want above all else are a cool drink and your paper and slippers for a half hour of relaxation before dinner. Little Johnnie, aged four or five, is around waiting to play baseball. You tell him, "Sorry, but I don't feel like baseball tonight; run and play somewhere else for a half hour while I read my paper." Then you get the drink out and get all settled comfortably with the paper.

Johnnie is playing around the room, bouncing his ball and a little unhappy. Of course, he does not say anything. Now it just happens—and I'm sure Johnnie did not intend it—but it does happen that Johnnie's ball bounces your way and tips over your drink!

There are all kinds of ways—some of them are not even conscious—in which we express our aggression when we are frustrated. Restriction of output, various kinds of "sabotage," waste, spoilage, and many other things happen on the job. Frequently these are simply symptoms, but yet they are an expression of people's reactions to feelings of frustration. Sometimes people are not even aware that they are being aggressive, but management has generally found out that these reactions to frustration defeat management's own purpose in one way or the other.

So, attempting to make people be docile, I believe, is an unrealistic approach. It is a philosophy that fundamentally will not work.

The Philosophy of Paternalism

Some managements made an altogether different attack on this problem. They said in effect, "Be good. If you're good, people out of loyalty and gratitude will do what you want them to do." Notice that the notion of docility is still there. The idea is that management has a job to do: to accomplish the organization's purpose through people. It can only accomplish that purpose if people do what they are told—if they are docile and accept orders.

The first group we talked about simply said, "If they won't, make them do it." The second group thought about it another way. The idea was, "Be good to them and they will do what you want them to." Out of this second group stems the whole philosophy of paternalism with which many of us are familiar.

Unfortunately, this philosophy has not worked too well either. When you simply give people things—which is what this philosophy promotes—it follows that they want more things: "Here is a lovely Santa Claus, who makes everything possible for me and gives me a lot of things I want. My attitude toward that Santa Claus is, come around again with your pack. If he doesn't, I'm frustrated by the fact that he hasn't given me some more."

People do not in general give their loyalties or their efforts out of gratitude; in fact, it makes them feel a little uncomfortable to be put in that dependent position. We have had several instances across the country of severe strikes and violent upheavals in companies that have been noted for their excessive paternalism. Employees who, to all intents and purposes, have everything, stand up in rebellion and say, "We don't want to be given things." Behind that is a certain feeling, perhaps, that it lowers their sense of importance to have somebody else decide what is good for them.

There is one other approach that has been characteristic of some managements. This approach is a compromise between the other two. It seems to me that it emerged during the last war, when management realized that a lot of tactics that had been used in the past did not seem to be working too well. Employees were pretty uppity and very hard to handle, particularly if the attempt was to make them docile. That compromise was essentially this: "Be firm, but fair; give them the wages and the benefits to which they are entitled, in terms of the community and the place in which you operate. Don't be tough, don't try to make them do what you tell them, but be firm. Draw a line somewhere and don't move beyond that line."

I do not believe that any company that has followed this philosophy will say it is the final answer to our problems of human relations. The reason it does not work too well is that it is a compromise between two fundamentally unworkable principles. Neither the "be good" nor the "be tough" philosophy will in itself accomplish the job. When you simply take part of each of them, you have not come up with any real answer to the problem.

Cooperation for Organizational Objectives

My belief is that we must shift our frame of reference, our way of looking at management's problems, in order to find even partial answers to the difficulties I have been describing. From my point of view, the key to the difficulty with the traditional philosophy of management lies in the notion of the necessity for docility—the notion that if people would only do what they were told we could get our job done well. Quite frankly, I do not believe that people will ever do what they are told. I believe that managements that try to approach their job in that frame of mind are inevitably going to get frustrated.

Let us start again by saying that management's job is to

get the organizational objective achieved: the production and sale of goods at a profit. But let us take a little different attitude. We do not regard people as a commodity now; we do not ask them to be docile. We say that management's task is to get people's cooperation, to create the conditions under which people will willingly and voluntarily work toward organizational objectives.

That may sound like an idealistic goal. However, if we could get even a majority of the people in an organization to work toward organizational objectives because they wanted to, management's job would be a very different job. I do not argue that this can be achieved today, tomorrow, or ten years from now; but I do argue that, if this is the goal toward which management directs its thinking, management will approach the day-to-day job in a very different way than if the goal is, "Make them do what they are told," or "Be good, and then they will do what they are told." It is a fundamentally different slant on management's job.

What are some of the conditions that management could create, or some of the problems that management could help to solve, if it took upon itself that task? It does not make any difference whether you are a supervisor at the first level, a manager in the middle, or the president on the top. The problem is to do your part of accomplishing the organizational objective. Let us suppose now that your attitude and philosophy are: "How can I get people voluntarily to want to work together toward the organization's objectives?"

In a way, what I am talking of is a little like the problem that an engineer faces when he is going to design a machine. He knows in advance the things he wants the machine to accomplish. Then, if he uses the right materials and puts them together in the right way, with enough skill on his part, he will eventually get a machine that works. Of course, that machine never works as well as the ideal of physical theory might indicate, because we always have friction (among other things) to cope with. However, we can approach the ideal. The same thing is true in designing a human organization. We may never get to the ideal, but if we have the ideal in mind we can hope at least to approach it.

I should like to make three or four points that seem to me to be pertinent if one adopts this different philosophy of attempting to get voluntary cooperation as a manager. The first is this rather simple but fundamental notion about human behavior: all human behavior is directed toward the satisfaction of needs. Life is a struggle for need satisfaction, extending from birth till death. In fact, when we cease trying to satisfy our needs, we *are* dead. Of all the kinds of needs, there are three that are crucially important to us as managers working with people in industry. First, there are the physical needs for such things as food, shelter, clothing, air, elimination, exercise, rest, and all of the biological necessities of the organism. They are obvious and they are important, of course.

Second, there is a cluster of needs that I like to call social. These grow out of the fact that we live in a highly interdependent society in which we no longer do things for ourselves. We no longer build our own houses, or make our own clothes, or grow our own food. We are dependent, all of us, on other people for getting our needs satisfied, and therefore it is inevitable that we should develop needs of a social sort. There is the need for companionship, the need for status among one's fellows, the desire to be regarded in the eyes of our associates as an acceptable person, and so on. These social needs work both ways—they are not only a "taking-in affair," but also a "giving-out affair." People get real enjoyment from behavior that is directed toward the group, and in helping the group to achieve its goals.

Finally, there is a group that I call egoistic needs, the needs that relate to the person himself. Such things as the need for achievement—to accomplish something, to solve a difficult task and be able to pat yourself on the chest and say, "I did that." Then there are the needs for knowledge, for creativity, for recognition and prestige in other people's eyes.

Need Satisfactions on the Job

These physical, social, and egoistic needs are the things that people are striving to satisfy throughout their lives, whether they may be on the job or off the job. The problem management has, if it is going to adopt this philosophy of voluntary cooperation, is to find ways in which behavior directed toward organizational purposes will provide satisfaction of such needs as these. When we make that explicit, and when we start to examine it, we will find that management has frequently missed some opportunities.

First and fundamentally, unless people believe down deep inside themselves that they can get their needs satisfied from the job to a reasonable degree, then they are not going to be willing to work for us voluntarily. They may do it out of fear, but not voluntarily. That notion of a kind of emotional security, or confidence that the job will provide opportunities for need satisfaction, is crucial in creating cooperation.

There is where the boss comes in, because it is the boss who tends to control those opportunities for need satisfaction. The boss controls wages and promotions. He controls the opportunity to "swing your cat a little bit" on your own job, to be creative, to solve problems, and to get knowledge. I must have a genuine confidence that he is going to give me the best break he can so that I can get my needs satisfied. Therefore, the first requirement is a basic confidence on the part of people in their managers. That is the foundation, and without it you have nothing.

The second point is a little less obvious, but I think it is equally important. The people that work for us spend about a third of their waking lives on the job. Consider how much in the way of real need satisfaction they get in the work situation itself, on the job. We pay them wages, but they cannot spend their wages at work; they have to go somewhere else to get that need satisfaction. We give them vacations, but they cannot enjoy their vacations at work. We give them pensions, but they cannot get that satisfaction while they work; they must retire and leave the job. As a matter of fact, when you go down the list of things that we provide people as means for need satisfaction from working, practically all of them are things that they can utilize for satisfaction only when they leave the job and go somewhere else.

Unless the job itself can be satisfying, unless there are opportunities right in the work situation to get fun out of working, we will never get people to direct their efforts voluntarily towards organizational goals. In fact, the reverse happens. Work becomes a kind of punishment they undergo in order to get those things they require for need satisfaction after they leave the job.

You, as management, frequently underestimate the importance of this problem for the people who work for you. Because of being in the management group, you automatically get a greater degree of need satisfaction in work itself. You have greater freedom, more opportunities for social satisfaction, more opportunities for achievement, for acquiring additional knowledge, for being creative. All of the things that can provide satisfaction at work are more available to you than they are to the fellow on the bottom. Even there, I think there is a gradient as one moves up the organizational ladder from the bottom to the top. The opportunities for having your work be fun, be enjoyable, be satisfying, get greater the higher up the line you go.

The third thought (the first was confidence, the second was on-the-job satisfaction) relates to a psychological law. Once again, I think you will recognize it in common-sense terms: behavior that leads to punishment or to lack of satisfaction tends to drop out. We call this the law of effect. Stop and examine for a moment how much of the behavior of the people working for you that results in need satisfaction for them is behavior directed toward organizational goals. The problem is to see to it that behavior that is directed toward organizational goals is satisfying to people, and that it is satisfying in proportion to the effort they put out toward organizational goals.

Are we set up that way? Do we run our departments that way? Well, consider wages and salaries. Is the person paid in general in such a fashion that the harder he works for the organization the more he gets? Perhaps so, in the long run through promotions and pay increases. That depends a lot on how the manager runs the wage-administration program. Does he really reward effort toward organizational purposes, or does he reward the employee who plays up to him, who is careful to consider the boss' prejudices? Does the boss play favorites? If he does, he is not rewarding behavior toward organizational goals.

In many instances, as I see the thing operate (and this is particularly true at the hourly wage level), the way you collect your day's wages is to stay employed. That's all. If you can keep from being fired, you get your wages. That forces the individual to the minimum of performance that he can get by with. The average worker today does not direct his energy toward organizational goals with the idea that if he does he can get promoted, because statistically he knows that his chances of promotion are pretty small. Some people are motivated that way; the great mass of people are not. Consequently, if we want their genuine cooperation, we must make sure that the need satisfaction we offer cannot be obtained merely by the minimum effort that enables them to stay employed.

When we turn to the other benefits we offer, the picture is even clearer. How do you get your vacation pay? How do you get your pension? How do you get your holidays? How do you get your insurance benefits? By working harder for the organization and helping to achieve organizational goals? No, not a bit of it. So long as you are employed —if you can keep from being fired—you will get them, just like death and taxes. Somewhere along the line we have to find ways (and I do not think they will be solely in the form of money returns) to see to it that people get genuine satisfaction out of directing their efforts toward organizational goals.

Through the utilization of ideas like the principle of consultative supervision, our subordinates can get the feeling of increased dignity, of achievement, of prestige, of social satisfaction. Those are important ways in which people can get satisfaction by working toward organizational goals. However, you, as managers, must provide those opportunities; they will not just happen.

One other point. There are big differences in the kinds of opportunities that can be provided for people to obtain need satisfaction. It is relatively easy to provide means (chiefly in the form of money) for need satisfaction—at least until the supply is exhausted. You cannot, however, provide people with a sense of achievement, or with knowledge, or with prestige. You can provide *opportunities* for them to obtain these satisfactions through efforts directed toward organization goals. What is even more important, the *supply of such opportunities*—unlike the supply of money—*is unlimited*.

This philosophy of management is not an easy one to practice. It offers, nevertheless, a challenge to all of us. It has one important virtue: it does not require the impossible task of making human beings docile, of creating conditions in which they will do what they are told without question or resistance. Management in the past has tried to do the impossible, partly because of a faulty conception of human behavior and human motivation. Today we can correct that error if we will.

PART TWO

■

LEADERSHIP

4

Conditions of Effective Leadership
in the Industrial Organization

THIS DISCUSSION of relationships among people at work is written from the point of view of dynamic psychology which, because of its origin in the clinic, directs attention to the whole individual living and interacting within a world of other individuals. Life, from the point of view of dynamic psychology, is a continuous striving to satisfy ever-changing needs in the face of obstacles. The work life is but a segment —although a large one—of the whole.

The Setting

Within this framework we shall examine some of the important forces and events in the work situation that aid or hinder the individual as he strives to satisfy his needs. First of all, we must recognize a fundamental fact: the direct

Reprinted from the *Journal of Consulting Psychology*, 1944, *8*, No. 2, 55–63.

impact of almost all these forces upon the individual is through the behavior of other people. This is obvious when we speak of an order from the boss, or pressures exerted by fellow workers to get the individual to join a union. It is perhaps less obvious when we speak of the impact of the business cycle, or the consequences of a fundamental technological change. Nevertheless, the direct influence of these forces on the individual—whether he is a worker or a plant manager—occurs through the medium of the actions of other people. We must include not only the easily observed actions of others, but the subtle, fleeting manifestations of attitude and emotion to which the individual reacts almost unconsciously.

For purposes of discussion we may arbitrarily divide the actions of other people that influence the individual in the work situation into three classes: actions of superiors, of subordinates, and of associates. We shall limit our attention mainly to the actions of superiors as they affect the subordinate in his striving to satisfy his needs. This relationship is logically prior to the others, and it is in many ways the most important human relationship in industry.

The fundamental characteristics of the subordinate-superior relationship are identical whether one talks of the worker and the supervisor, the assistant superintendent and the superintendent, or the vice president and the president. There are, to be sure, differences in the content of the relationship, and in the relative importance of its characteristics, at different levels of the industrial organization. The underlying aspects, however, are common to all levels.

The Dependence of the Subordinate

The outstanding characteristic of the relationship between the subordinate and his superiors is his dependence upon them for the satisfaction of his needs. Industry in our civilization is organized along authoritative lines. In a fundamental and pervasive sense, the subordinate is dependent upon his superiors for his job, for the continuity of his employment, for promotion with its accompanying satisfactions in the form of increased pay, responsibility, and prestige, and for a host of other personal and social satisfactions to be obtained in the work situation.

This dependence is not adequately recognized in our culture. For one thing, it is not consistent with some of our basic social values. The emphasis is usually placed upon the importance of the subordinate's own effects in achieving the satisfaction of his needs. Nevertheless, the dependence is real, and subordinates are not unaware of it. Among workers, surveys of attitudes invariably place "fair treatment by superiors" toward the top of the list of factors influencing job satisfaction.[1,2] And the extent to which unions have attempted to place restrictions upon management's authority reflects not only a desire for power but a conscious attempt to reduce the dependence of workers upon their bosses.[3,4]

Psychologically, the dependence of the subordinate upon his superiors is a fact of extraordinary significance, partly because of its emotional similarity to the dependence characteristic of another earlier relationship: that between the child and his parents. The similarity is more than an analogy. The adult subordinate's dependence upon his superiors actually reawakens certain emotions and attitudes which were

[1] Harold B. Bergen, "Measuring Attitudes and Morale in Wartime." *The Conference Board Management Record*, 1942, *4*, No. 4, 101–104.

[2] Robert N. McMurry, "Management Mentalities and Worker Reactions." *Advanced Management*, 1942, 7, No. 4, 165–172.

[3] Robert R. R. Brooks, *When Labor Organizes*. New Haven: Yale University Press, 1938.

[4] Twentieth Century Fund, *How Collective Bargaining Works: A Survey of Experience in Leading American Industries*. New York: The Fund, 1942.

part of his childhood relationship with his parents, and which apparently have long since been outgrown. The adult is usually unaware of the similarity, because most of this complex of childhood emotions has been repressed. Although the emotions influence his behavior, they are not accessible to consciousness under ordinary circumstances.

Superficially it may seem absurd to compare these two relationships, but one cannot observe human behavior in industry without being struck by the fundamental similarity between them. Space limitations prevent elaboration of this point here, in spite of its great importance.[5]

There are certain inevitable consequences of the dependence of the subordinate upon his superiors. The success or failure of the relationship depends on the way in which these consequences are handled. An understanding of them provides a more useful basis than the usual "rules of thumb" for a consideration of problems of industrial relations. These consequences of the dependence of the subordinate will be discussed under two main headings: (1) the necessity for security in the work situation, and (2) the necessity for self-realization.

The Necessity for Security

Subordinates will struggle to protect themselves against real or imagined threats to the satisfaction of their needs in the work situation. Analysis of this protective behavior suggests that the actions of superiors are frequently perceived as the

[5] The relevant literature is vast. A fair introduction to it may be obtained through the following: Walter C. Langer, *Psychology and Human Living*. New York: D. Appleton-Century, 1943; A. H. Maslow and Bela Mittelmann, *Principles of Abnormal Psychology*. New York: Harper and Brothers, 1941; John Dollard, Leonard W. Doob, et al., *Frustration and Aggression*. New Haven: Yale University Press, 1939; John Levy and Ruth Monroe, *The Happy Family*. New York: Alfred A. Knopf, 1941.

source of the threats.[6] Before subordinates can believe that it is possible to satisfy their wants in the work situation, they must acquire a convincing sense of security in their dependent relationship to their superiors.

Management has recognized the financial aspects of this need for security, and has attempted to provide for it by means of employee retirement plans, health and accident insurance, the encouragement of employee credit unions, and even guaranteed annual wages.[7] However this recognition does not get at the heart of the problem: the personal dependence of the subordinate upon the judgments and decisions of his superior.

Labor unions have attacked the problem more directly in their attempts to obtain rules governing promotions and layoffs, grievance procedures, arbitration provisions, and protection against arbitrary changes in work loads and rates.[8,9] One important purpose of such "protective" features in union contracts is to restrict superiors in the making of decisions that, *from the worker's point of view*, are arbitrary and threatening. They help to provide the subordinate with

[6] Cf., for example, the detailed observation of the "bank-wiring" group at the Hawthorne Plant of Western Electric, reported in Chaps. 17–23 of F. J. Roethlisberger and W. J. Dickson, *Management and the Worker*. Cambridge, Mass.: Harvard University Press, 1939. For evidence at another level of the industrial organization, see Conrad M. Arensberg and Douglas McGregor, "Determination of Morale in an Industrial Company." *Applied Anthropology*, 1942, *1*, No. 2, 12–34.

[7] Discussions of plans for financial security will be found in the research reports of the National Industrial Conference Board and the Personnel Division of the American Management Association, and in the publications of the Policyholders' Service Bureau of the Metropolitan Life Insurance Company.

[8] Cf. U.S. Department of Labor, Bureau of Labor Statistics, *Union Agreement Provisions*. Bulletin No. 686. Washington, D.C.: Government Printing Office, 1942.

[9] Sumner H. Slichter, *Union Policies and Industrial Management*. Washington, D.C.: The Brookings Institution, 1941.

a measure of security despite his dependence on his superiors.

The Conditions of Security: An Atmosphere of Approval

There are three major aspects of the subordinate-superior relationship—*at any level of the organization*—that affect the security of the subordinate. The most important of these is what we may term the "atmosphere" created by the superior.[10] This atmosphere is revealed not by what the superior does, but by the manner in which he does it, and by his underlying attitude toward his subordinates. It is relatively independent of the strictness of the superior's discipline or the standards of performance that he demands.

A foreman who had unwittingly created such an atmosphere attempted to establish a rule that union officials should obtain his permission when they left the job to meet with higher management and report to him when they returned. This entirely reasonable action aroused intense resentment, although the same rule was readily accepted by union officials in another part of the plant. The specific actions were unimportant except in terms of the background against which the subordinates perceived them: an atmosphere of disapproval in the one case and of approval in the other.

Security for subordinates is possible only when they know they have the genuine approval of their superior. If the atmosphere is equivocal, or one of disapproval, they can have no assurance that their needs will be satisfied, *regardless of*

[10] The vital importance of this attitude in familial superior-subordinate relationships is stressed everywhere in the literature of dynamic psychology. See, for example, J. McV. Hunt, *Personality and the Behavior Disorders*. New York: The Ronald Press, 1944, Vol. II.

what they do. In the absence of a genuine attitude of approval, subordinates feel threatened, fearful, insecure. Even neutral and innocuous actions of the superior are regarded with suspicion. Effective discipline is impossible, high standards of performance cannot be maintained, "sabotage" of the superior's efforts is almost inevitable. Resistance, antagonism, and ultimately open rebellion are the consequences.

The Conditions of Security: Knowledge

The second requirement for the subordinate's security is knowledge. *He must know what is expected of him.* Otherwise he may, through errors of commission or omission, interfere with the satisfaction of his own needs. There are several kinds of knowledge that the subordinate requires.

1. *Knowledge of over-all company policy and management philosophy.* Security is impossible in a world of shifting foundations. This fact was convincingly demonstrated—to management in particular—during the first few months of the existence of the War Labor Board. The cry for a national labor policy was frequently heard. "Without it we don't know how to act." Likewise, subordinates in the individual company require a knowledge of the broad policy and philosophy of top management.[11]

2. *Knowledge of procedures, rules, and regulations.* Without this knowledge, the subordinate can only learn by trial and error, and the threat of punishment because of innocent infractions hangs always over his head.[12]

[11] A few employee "handbooks" demonstrate an awareness of this point. See, for example, *Employee Relations in General Foods.* 2nd ed. New York: General Foods Corporation, May 19, 1941.

[12] This is the usually recognized reason for the publication of employee handbooks. Cf. Alexander R. Heron, *Sharing Information with Employees.* Stanford University, Calif.: Stanford University Press, 1942.

3. *Knowledge of the requirements of the subordinate's own job—his duties, responsibilities, and place in the organization.* It is surprising how often subordinates (particularly within the management organization) are unable to obtain this essential knowledge. Lacking it, one can never be sure when to make a decision, or when to refer the matter to someone else; when to act or when to "pass the buck." [13] The potential dangers in this kind of insecurity are apparent upon the most casual consideration.

4. *Knowledge of the personal peculiarities of the subordinate's immediate superior.* The good salesman never approaches a new prospect without learning all he can about his interests, habits, prejudices, and opinions. The subordinate must sell *himself* to his superior, and consequently such knowledge is indispensable to him. Does the boss demand initiative and originality, or does he want to make all the decisions himself? What are the unpardonable sins, the things this superior never forgives or forgets? What are his soft spots, and what are his blind spots? There can be no security for the subordinate until he has discovered the answers to these questions.

5. *Knowledge by the subordinate of the superior's opinion of his performance.* Where do I stand? How am I doing? To know where you stand in the eyes of your superiors is to know what you must do in order to satisfy your needs.[14] Lacking this knowledge, the subordinate can have, at best, only a false sense of security.

[13] Donaldson Brown, "Industrial Management as a National Resource." *The Conference Board Management Record*, 1943, 5, No. 4, 142–148.

[14] This, of course, is the reason for merit rating plans. Cf. National Industrial Conference Board, Inc., *Employee Rating. Methods of Appraising Ability, Efficiency and Potentialities*. Studies in Personnel Policy No. 39. New York: N.I.C.B., 1941.

6. *Advance knowledge of changes that may affect the subordinate.* Resistance to change is a common phenomenon among employees in industry.[15],[16],[17] One of the fundamental reasons is the effect of unpredictable changes upon security. If the subordinate knows that he will always be given adequate warning of changes, and an understanding of the reasons for them, he does not fear them half so much. Conversely, the normal inertia of human habits is tremendously reinforced when one must be forever prepared against unforeseen changes in policy, rules, methods of work, or even in the continuity of employment and wages.

It is not necessary to turn to industry for evidence in support of the principles outlined above. Everywhere in our world today we see the consequences of the insecurity caused by our inability to know what we need to know in order to insure even partially the satisfaction of our needs. Knowledge is power, primarily because it decreases dependence upon the unknown and unpredictable.

The Conditions of Security: Consistent Discipline

The third requirement for the subordinate's security in his relationship of dependence on his superiors is that of consistent discipline. It is a fact often unrecognized that discipline may take the form of positive support for "right" actions as well as criticism and punishment for "wrong"

[15] Roethlisberger and Dickson, *op. cit.*

[16] Douglas McGregor and Irving Knickerbocker, "Industrial Relations and National Defense: A Challenge to Management." *Personnel*, 1941, *18*, No. 1, 49–63.

[17] Slichter, *op. cit.*, Chaps. 7–9.

ones. The subordinate, in order to be secure, requires consistent discipline in both senses.[18]

He requires, first of all, the strong and willing backing of his superiors for those actions that are in accord with what is expected of him. There is much talk among some managements about superiors who fail to "back up" their subordinates. The insecurity that arises when a subordinate does not know under what conditions he will be backed up leads him to "keep his neck pulled in" at all times. Buck passing and its consequent frictions and resentment are inevitable under such circumstances.

Given a clear knowledge of what is expected of him, the subordinate requires, in addition, definite assurance that he will have the unqualified support of his superiors so long as his actions are consistent with those policies and are taken within the limits of his responsibility. Only then can he have the security and confidence that will enable him to do his job well.

At the same time the subordinate must know that failure to live up to his responsibilities, or to observe the rules that are established, will result in punishment. Every individual has many wants that conflict with the demands of his job. If he knows that breaking the rules to satisfy these wants will *almost inevitably* result in the frustration of his vital long-range needs, self-discipline will be less difficult. If, on the other hand, discipline is inconsistent and uncertain, he may be unnecessarily denying himself satisfaction by obeying the rules. The insecurity born of uncertainty and of guilt, which is inevitably a consequence of lax discipline, is unpleasant and painful for the subordinate.

[18] This, of course, is simply the well known principle underlying all theories of learning. We need not discuss here its many complicated features.

What frequently happens is this. The superior, in trying to be a "good fellow," fails to maintain discipline and to obtain the standards of performance that are necessary. His subordinates—human beings striving to satisfy their needs— "take advantage of the situation." The superior then begins to disapprove of his subordinates (in spite of the fact that he is to blame for their behavior). Perhaps he "cracks down" on them, perhaps he simply grows more and more critical and disapproving. In either event, because he has failed to establish consistent discipline *in an atmosphere of genuine approval*, they are threatened. The combination of guilt and insecurity on the part of the subordinates leads easily to antagonism and, therefore, to further actions of which the superior disapproves. Thus a vicious circle is set up in which disapproval → antagonistic acts → more disapproval → more antagonistic acts. In the end it becomes extremely difficult to remedy a situation of this kind, because both superior and subordinates have a chip-on-the-shoulder attitude which must be abolished before the relationship can improve.

Every subordinate, then, requires the security of knowing that he can count on the firm support of his superiors for doing what is "right," and firm pressure (even punishment) to prevent his doing what is "wrong." *But this discipline must be established and maintained in an atmosphere of approval.* Otherwise, the subordinate's suspicion and resentment of his superiors will lead to the opposite reaction from the desired one. A mild degree of discipline is sufficient in an atmosphere of approval; even the most severe discipline will in the end be unsuccessful in an atmosphere of disapproval. The behavior of the people in the occupied countries of Europe today provides a convincing demonstration of this psychological principle.

The Necessity for Independence

When the subordinate has achieved a reasonable degree of genuine security in his relationship to his superiors, he will begin to seek ways of utilizing more fully his capacities and skills, of achieving through his own efforts a larger degree of satisfaction from his work. Given security, the subordinate seeks to develop himself. This *active* search for independence is constructive and healthy. It is collaborative and friendly, yet genuinely self-assertive.

If, on the other hand, the subordinate feels that his dependence on his superiors is extreme, and if he lacks security,[19] he will fight blindly for freedom. This *reactive* struggle for independence is founded on fear and hatred. It leads to friction and strife, and it tends to perpetuate itself, because it interferes with the development of an atmosphere of approval that is essential to security.

These two fundamentally opposite ways in which subordinates seek to acquire independence have entirely different consequences. Since we are concerned with the conditions of the successful subordinate-superior relationship, we shall emphasize the active rather than the reactive striving for independence.[20]

The Conditions of Active Independence

Participation

One of the most important conditions of the subordinate's growth and development centers around his opportunities to express his ideas and to contribute his suggestions before

[19] It is the *subordinate's own feelings* and not the "objective" facts that are vital in this connection.

[20] A. H. Maslow, "The Authoritarian Character Structure." *The Journal of Social Psychology*, 1943, *18*, 401–411.

his superiors take action on matters that involve him.[21,22] Through participation of this kind, he becomes more and more aware of his superiors' problems, and he obtains a genuine satisfaction in knowing that his opinions and ideas are given consideration in the search for solutions.[23]

Participation of this kind is fairly prevalent in the upper levels of industrial organizations. It is often entirely lacking further down the line. Some people insist that the proponents of participation at the lower levels of industry are unrealistic idealists. However, there are highly successful instances in existence of "consultative supervision," [24] "multiple management," [25] and "union-management cooperation." [26] The important point is that participation cannot be successful unless the conditions of security are adequately met. Many failures among the currently popular Labor-Management Production Drive Committees can be traced directly to this fundamental fact that active independence cannot be achieved in the absence of adequate security.[27,28]

[21] The work of Kurt Lewin and his students at the University of Iowa on group dynamics is relevant to this whole discussion, but it is especially pertinent to this matter of participation. Cf. K. Lewin, R. Lippitt, and S. K. Escalona, "Studies in Topological and Vector Psychology I." *University of Iowa Studies in Child Welfare*, 1940, *16*, No. 3.

[22] Alex Bavelas, "Morale and the Training of Leaders." In Goodwin Watson (Ed.), *Civilian Morale*. Second Yearbook of the Society for the Psychological Study of Social Issues. Boston: Houghton Mifflin, 1942.

[23] The fear is often expressed that subordinates, given the slightest opportunity, will seek to usurp their superiors' "prerogatives." Actually, such attempts are symptomatic of the *reactive* struggle for independence. These fears are groundless when subordinates are given adequate security.

[24] H. H. Carey, "Consultative Supervision and Management." *Personnel*, 1942, *18*, No. 5, 286–295.

[25] Charles P. McCormick, *Multiple Management*. New York: Harper and Brothers, 1938.

[26] Clinton S. Golden and Harold J. Ruttenberg, *The Dynamics of Industrial Democracy*. New York: Harper and Brothers, 1942.

[27] "Survey of the Labor-Management Production Drive." *Mill and Factory*, 1942, *30*, No. 6, 57–60.

[28] "Are War Production Drives Worth While?" *Factory Management and Maintenance*, 1942, *100*, No. 10, 74–80.

There is a real challenge and a deep satisfaction for the subordinate who is given the opportunity to aid in the solution of the difficult but fascinating problems that arise daily in any industrial organization. The superior who, having provided security for his subordinates, encourages them to accept this challenge and to strive *with him* to obtain this satisfaction, is almost invariably surprised at the fruitfulness of the results. The president of one company remarked, after a few management conferences designed to encourage this kind of participation, that he had never before realized in considering his problems how many alternative possibilities were available, nor how inadequate had been the knowledge upon which he based his decisions. Contrary to the usual opinion, this discovery is as likely at the bottom of an organization as at the top, once the initial feelings of inadequacy and hesitancy among workers are overcome.[29]

The genuine collaboration among all the members of an industrial organization that is eulogized by "impractical idealists" is actually quite possible. But it can begin to emerge only when the mechanisms of genuine participation become an established part of the organization routines.

Responsibility

A corollary of the desire for participation is a desire for responsibility. It is another manifestation of the active search for independence. Insecure or rebellious subordinates—seeking independence in the reactive sense—do not accept responsibility. They are seeking freedom, not the opportunity for self-realization and development.

The willingness to assume responsibility is a genuine mat-

[29] Golden and Ruttenberg, *op. cit.*, Chap. 9.

urational phenomenon. Just as children cannot grasp the meaning of the algebraic use of symbols until their intellectual development has reached a certain level, so subordinates cannot accept responsibility until they have achieved a certain degree of emotional security in their relationship to their superiors. Then they want it. They accept it with obvious pleasure and pride. And if it is given to them gradually, so that they are not suddenly made insecure again by too great a load of it, they will continue to accept more and more.

The process of granting responsibility to subordinates is a delicate one. There are vast individual differences in tolerance for the inevitable pressures and insecurities attendant upon the acceptance of responsibility. Some subordinates seem to be content to achieve a high degree of security without independence. Others thrive on the risks and the dangers of being "on their own." However, there are few subordinates whose capabilities in this direction are fully realized. It is unwise to attribute the absence of a desire for responsibility to the individual's personality alone until one has made certain that his relationship to his superiors is genuinely secure.

Many superiors are themselves so insecure that they cannot run the risk of being responsible for their subordinates' mistakes. Often they are unconsciously afraid to have capable and developing subordinates. The delegation of responsibility, as well as its acceptance, requires a confident and secure relationship with one's superiors.[30]

[30] Irving Knickerbocker and Douglas McGregor, "Union-Management Cooperation: A Psychological Analysis." *Personnel,* 1942, *19,* No. 3, 530–533 (reprinted on pp. 83–113 of this volume).

The Right of Appeal

There are occasions when subordinates differ radically but sincerely with their superiors on important questions. Unless the superior follows an "appeasement" policy (which in the end will cost him his subordinates' respect), there exists in such disagreement the possibility of an exaggerated feeling of dependence and helplessness in the minds of the subordinates. They disagree for reasons that seem *to them* sound; yet they must defer to the judgment of one person whom they know to be fallible.

If these occasions are too frequent, the subordinates will be blocked in their search for independence, and they may readily revert to a reactive struggle. The way out of the dilemma is to provide the subordinate with a mechanism for appealing his superior's decisions to a higher level of the organization. The subordinate can then have at hand a check upon the correctness and fairness of his superior's actions. His feeling of independence is thereby increased.

This is one of the justifications for an adequate grievance procedure for workers.[31,32] All too often, however, there is no similar mechanism provided for members of management. To be sure, in the absence of a union it is difficult to safeguard the individual against retaliative measures by his immediate superior, but it is possible to guarantee a reasonable degree of protection.

If the relationship between subordinate and superior is a successful one, the right of appeal may rarely be exercised. Nevertheless, the awareness that it is there to be used when

[31] Solomon Barkin, "Unions and Grievances." *Personnel Journal*, 1943, 22, No. 2, 38–48.

[32] U.S. Department of Labor, Division of Labor Standards, *Settling Plant Grievances*. Bulletin No. 60. Washington, D.C.: Government Printing Office, 1943.

needed provides the subordinate with a feeling of independence which is not otherwise possible.

Summary

The subordinate in the industrial organization is dependent for the satisfaction of many of his vital needs upon the behavior and attitudes of his superiors. He requires, therefore, a feeling of confidence that he can satisfy his needs if he does what is expected of him. Given this security, he requires opportunities for self-realization and development.

Among the conditions influencing the subordinate's feelings of security are: (1) an "atmosphere" of approval, (2) knowledge of what is expected of him and of how well he is measuring up to these expectations, (3) forewarning of changes that may affect him, and (4) consistent discipline in the form of both backing when he is "right" and punishment when he is "wrong."

The conditions under which the subordinate can realize his own potentialities include: (1) an adequate sense of security in relation to his superiors, (2) opportunities to participate in the solution of problems and in the discussion of actions that may affect him, (3) the opportunity to assume responsibility as he becomes ready for it, and (4) the right of appeal over the head of his immediate superior.

These conditions are minimal. Upon their fulfillment in some degree rests the success or failure of the subordinate-superior relationship at every level of the industrial organization from that of the vice president to that of the worker.

5

On Leadership

IN A FEW WEEKS I shall preside over the commencement exercises of Antioch's 101st year. Then, with mixed feelings, I shall become an ex-president of one of the most exciting educational institutions in America.

On the one hand, I am eager to renew direct acquaintance with students in the classroom and to rejoin my colleagues in the planning and execution of research on the problems of human relations in industry. On the other hand, I am reluctant to leave the wonderful people of Antioch who have provided me with such a rich experience during the past six years. They have taught me a new conception of education and a new appreciation of the potentialities of young people.

It will require time to think back over the many events that have been crowded into these few years and to draw a proper meaning from them. However, two related convictions have developed slowly but steadily out of this experience. Perhaps they are worth brief elaboration.

This essay appeared in *Antioch Notes*, May 1, 1954, *31*, No. 9.

The Boss Must Boss

The first is a conviction that has been derived from my personal struggle with the role of college president. Before coming to Antioch I had observed and worked with top executives as an adviser in a number of organizations. I thought I knew how they felt about their responsibilities and what led them to behave as they did. I even thought that I could create a role for myself that would enable me to avoid some of the difficulties they encountered. I was wrong! It took the direct experience of becoming a line executive, and meeting personally the problems involved, to teach me what no amount of observation of other people could have taught.

I believed, for example, that a leader could operate successfully as a kind of adviser to his organization. I thought I could avoid being a "boss." Unconsciously, I suspect, I hoped to duck the unpleasant necessity of making difficult decisions, of taking the responsibility for one course of action among many uncertain alternatives, of making mistakes and taking the consequences. I thought that maybe I could operate so that everyone would like me—that "good human relations" would eliminate all discord and disagreement.

I could not have been more wrong. It took a couple of years, but I finally began to realize that a leader cannot avoid the exercise of authority any more than he can avoid responsibility for what happens to his organization. In fact, it is a major function of the top executive to take on his own shoulders the responsibility for resolving the uncertainties that are always involved in important decisions. Moreover, since no important decision ever pleases everyone in the organization, he must also absorb the displeasure, and sometimes severe hostility, of those who would have taken a different course.

A colleague recently summed up what my experience has taught me in these words: "A good leader must be tough enough to win a fight, but not tough enough to kick a man when he is down." This notion is not in the least inconsistent with humane, democratic leadership. Good human relations develop out of strength, not of weakness.

I am still trying to understand and practice what is implied in my colleague's statement.

The Fight against Bigotry

The second conviction relates to institutional rather than personal leadership. It emerged from direct experience with the antiintellectual attitudes, the suspicion, the fear, the damning accusations that characterize our life today. National and international tensions make us wary of nonconformity everywhere. It is an easy, popular pastime to link nonconformity with "Communist tendencies."

Our colleges and universities, Antioch among them, are frequently attacked by those who cannot countenance any views but their own. Because such attacks are persistent and melodramatic, a great many sensible people erroneously conclude that "where there is smoke, there must be fire." As a result, irreparable damage is often done to individuals and to organizations.

Antioch is a small college. It has a teaching faculty of about 75 people. After six years, I can say with some assurance that I know my faculty. I am convinced that there are no Communists, or near Communists, among them.

There is no educational institution in America more intimately interwoven with free-enterprise ideals. Our work-study plan is based on belief in our American economic system. Our college government is completely patterned on the American principles of representative government. The college has been a seedbed for many successful private enterprises. It is currently engaged in a major "risk-capital" venture: the operation of a multimillion dollar shopping center in Florida. These things are evidence of our faith in the American way.

But there are other facts, less well understood, about Antioch. For sound educational reasons, we try to recruit a student body that is representative of various geographic regions, various national and ethnic groups. And on our campus we do not differentiate among people because of the color of their skin or their religious affiliation. This is regarded by many as a radical policy, and probably Communist inspired.

We value the individual at Antioch. We think that he should have the freedom to grow intellectually according to his own abilities. We do not challenge his right to disagree, or to act on the basis of his beliefs, provided only that he acts openly in accord with the principles of democracy, and with honesty and integrity.

But these values, absolutely essential to any educational program worthy of the name, are widely distrusted today. If a college permits, let alone encourages, the right of disagreement, it is quickly accused of being under Communist influence.

I am no longer willing to take a defensive position with respect to these things. I am on the offensive. Antioch's philosophy, like that of colleges and universities throughout the country, is in accord with the fundamental principles of Christian ethics and of the Constitution of the United States. Its policies and procedures are openly developed through a system of representative government. It is doing a fine job of maintaining our American traditions and at the same time guarding against subversive infiltration. There is no reason whatever for Antioch to apologize to anyone for its personnel, its policies, or its practices.

It was, therefore, a source of satisfaction to me when the Antioch trustees this month gave unanimous expression to the following statement:

As members of the Board of Trustees of Antioch College, we are aware of the unnatural pressures that are brought against institutions of learning today. We wish to reaffirm our confidence in the administration, faculty, and student body of Antioch College. As loyal Americans, we believe that freedom of inquiry and belief by responsible scholars is essential to the moral health and spiritual progress of the nation. We commend Antioch College for the reasonableness with which it is preserving decent traditions of human relations. We urge the administration, faculty, and students to maintain intact their devotion to democratic principles against that golden day when Americans will no longer fear or distrust each other.

My second conviction thus relates also to leadership, but in an institutional rather than a personal sense: it is the business of colleges and universities to create a climate within which freedom of responsible inquiry and belief can flourish. These institutions must be tough enough to win the fight against whatever forces seek to destroy this freedom.

The college must lead, or the ideals of our founding fathers, and of thoughtful people everywhere, will wither away.

6

An Analysis of Leadership

ARE SUCCESSFUL MANAGERS born or "made"? Does success as a manager rest on the possession of a certain core of abilities and traits, or are there many combinations of characteristics that can result in successful industrial leadership? Is managerial leadership—or its potential—a property of the individual, or is it a term for describing a relationship between people? Will the managerial job 20 years from now require the same basic abilities and personality traits as it does today?

Knowledge gained from research in the social sciences sheds light on these and other questions relevant to leadership in industry. It does not provide final, definitive answers. There is much yet to be learned. But the accumulated evidence points with high probability toward certain ones among a number of possible assumptions.

The material in this article is from the book, *The Human Side of Enterprise*, by Douglas McGregor, published by McGraw-Hill Book Company, New York, 1960. The article appeared in *The Technology Review*, 1960, *62*, No. 9, 39–41, 64.

It is quite unlikely that there is a single basic pattern of abilities and personality traits characteristic of all leaders. The personality characteristics of the leader are not unimportant, but those that are essential differ considerably depending upon the circumstances. The requirements for successful political leadership are different from those for industrial management or military or educational leadership. Failure is as frequent as success in transfers of leaders from one type of social institution to another.

Even within a single institution such as industry, different circumstances require different leadership characteristics. Comparisons of successful industrial leaders in different historical periods, in different cultures, in different industries, or even in different companies have made this fairly obvious. The leadership requirements of a young, struggling company, for example, are quite different from those of a large, well-established firm.

Within the individual company different functions (sales, finance, production) demand rather different abilities and skills of leadership. Managers who are successful in one function are sometimes, but by no means always, successful in another. The same is true of leadership at different organizational levels. Every successful foreman would not make a successful president (or vice versa). Yet each may be an effective leader.

On the other hand, leaders who differ notably in abilities and traits are sometimes equally successful when they succeed each other in a given situation. Within rather wide limits, weaknesses in certain characteristics can be compensated by strength in others. This is particularly evident in partnerships and executive teams in which leadership functions are, in fact, shared. The very idea of the team implies different and supplementary patterns of abilities among the members.

Many characteristics that have been alleged to be essential to the leader turn out not to differentiate the successful leader from the unsuccessful ones. In fact, some of these—integrity, ambition, judgment, for example—are to be found not merely in the leader, but in any successful member of an organization.

Leadership Is a Relationship

There are at least four major variables now known to be involved in leadership: (1) the characteristics of the leader; (2) the attitudes, needs, and other personal characteristics of the followers; (3) the characteristics of the organization, such as its purpose, its structure, the nature of the task to be performed; and (4) the social, economic, and political milieu. The personal characteristics required for effective performance as a leader vary, depending on the other factors.

This is an important research finding. *It means that leadership is not a property of the individual, but a complex relationship among these variables*. The old argument over whether the leader makes history or history makes the leader is resolved by this conception. Both assertions are true within limits.

The relationship between the leader and the situation is essentially circular. Organization structure and policy, for example, are established by top management. Once established, they set limits on the leadership patterns that will be acceptable within the company. However, influences from above (a change in top management with an accompanying change in philosophy), from below (following recognition of a union and adjustment to collective bargaining, for example), or from outside (social legislation, changes in the market, etc.) bring about changes in these organizational characteristics. Some of these may lead to a redefinition of

acceptable leadership patterns. The changes that occurred
in the leadership of the Ford Motor Company after Henry
Ford I retired provide a dramatic illustration.

The same is true of the influence of the broader milieu.
The social values, the economic and political conditions, the
general standard of living, the level of education of the
population, and other factors characteristic of the late 1800's
had much to do with the kinds of people who were successful as industrial leaders during that era. Those men in turn
helped to shape the nature of the industrial environment.
Their influence affected the character of our society profoundly.

Today, industry requires a very different type of industrial leader from what was needed in 1900. Similarly, today's
leaders are helping to shape industrial organizations that tomorrow will require people quite different from themselves.

Conformity Is Rewarded

An important point with respect to these situational influences on leadership is that they operate selectively—in subtle
and unnoticed as well as obvious ways—to reward conformity with acceptable patterns of behavior and to punish
deviance from these. The differing situations from company
to company, and from unit to unit within a company, each
have their selective consequences. The observable managerial "types" in certain companies are illustrative of this
phenomenon. One consequence of this selectivity is the
tendency to "weed out" deviant individuals, some of whom
might nevertheless become effective, perhaps outstanding,
leaders.

Even if there is no single universal pattern of characteristics of the leader, it is conceivable at least that there might

be certain universal characteristics *of the relationship* between the leader and the other situational factors that are essential for optimum organized human effort in all situations. This is doubtful. Consider, for example, the relationship of an industrial manager with a group of native employees in an underdeveloped country, on the one hand, and with a group of United States workmen who are members of a well-established international union, on the other. Moreover, even if research finally indicates that there are such universal requirements of the relationship, there will still be more than one way of achieving them. For example, if "mutual confidence" between the leader and the led is a universal requirement, it is obvious that there are many ways of developing and maintaining this confidence.

It does not follow from these considerations that any individual can become a successful leader in a given situation. It does follow that successful leadership is not dependent on the possession of a single universal pattern of inborn traits and abilities. It seems likely that leadership potential (considering the tremendous variety of situations for which leadership is required) is broadly rather than narrowly distributed in the population.

Research findings to date suggest that it is more fruitful to consider leadership as a relationship between the leader and the situation than as a universal pattern of characteristics possessed by certain people. The differences in requirements for successful leadership in different situations are more striking than the similarities. Moreover, research studies emphasize the importance of leadership skills and attitudes that can be acquired and are, therefore, not inborn characteristics of the individual.

It has often happened in the physical sciences that what was once believed to be an inherent property of objects—

gravity, for example, or electrical "magnetism," or mass—has turned out to be a complex relationship between internal and external factors. The same thing happens in the social sciences, and leadership is but one example.

Implications for Management

What is the practical relevance for management of these findings of social science research in the field of leadership? First, if we accept the point of view that leadership consists of a relationship between the leader, his followers, the organization, and the social milieu, and if we recognize that these situational factors are subject to substantial changes with time, we must recognize that we cannot predict the personal characteristics of the managerial resources that an organization will require a decade or two hence. Even if we can list the positions to be filled, we cannot define very adequately the essential characteristics of the people who will be needed in those situations at that time. *One of management's major tasks, therefore, is to provide a heterogeneous supply of human resources from which individuals can be selected to fill a variety of specific but unpredictable needs.*

This is a blow to those who have hoped that the outcome of research would be to provide them with methods by which they could select today the top management of tomorrow. It is a boon to those who have feared the consequences of the "crown prince" approach to management development. It carries other practical implications of some importance.

With the modern emphasis on career employment and promotion from within, management must pay more than casual attention to its recruitment practices. It would seem logical that this process should tap a variety of sources: liberal arts as well as technical graduates, small colleges as well as big universities, institutions in different geographic regions, etc. It may be necessary, moreover, to look carefully at the criteria for selection of college recruits if heterogeneity is a goal. The college senior who graduates in the top 10 per cent of his class may come from a narrow segment of the range of potential leaders for industry. What of the student who has, perhaps for reasons unrelated to intellectual capacity, graduated in the middle of his class because he got A's in some subjects and C's and D's in others? What of the student whose academic achievement was only average because the education system never really challenged him?

As a matter of fact, there is not much evidence that high academic achievement represents a necessary characteristic for industrial leadership. There may be a positive correlation, but it is not large enough to provide a basis for a recruitment policy. In fact, more than one president of the United States would have been passed over at graduation by any management recruiter who relied on this correlation! It may be, on the contrary, that the *intellectual* capacity required for effective leadership in many industrial management positions is no greater than that required for graduation from a good college. Of course, there are positions requiring high intellectual capacity, but it does not follow that there is a one-to-one correlation between this characteristic and success as an industrial leader. (This question of intellectual capacity is, of course, only one reason why industry seeks the bulk of its potential managerial resources among college graduates today. There are other factors involved: confidence and social poise, skill acquired through participation in extracurricular activities, personal ambition and drive, etc. These, however, are relatively independent of class standing.)

It may be argued that intellectual *achievement*, as measured by consistently high grades in all subjects, is evidence of motivation and willingness to work. Perhaps it is—in the academic setting—but it is also evidence of willingness to conform to the quite arbitrary demands of the educational system. There is little reason for assuming that high motivation and hard work in school are the best predictors for motivation and effort in later life. There are a good many examples to the contrary.

Development Program Requirements

A second implication from research findings about leadership is that a management development program should involve many people within the organization rather than a select few. The fact that some companies have been reasonably successful in developing a selected small group of managerial trainees may well be an artifact—an example of the operation of the "self-fulfilling prophecy." If these companies had been equally concerned to develop managerial talent within a much broader sample, they might have accomplished this purpose with no greater percentage of failures. And, if the generalizations above are sound, they would have had a richer, more valuable pool of leadership resources to draw on as a result.

Third, management should have as a goal the development of the unique capacities and potentialities of each individual rather than common objectives for all participants. This is a purpose that is honored on paper much more than in practice. It is difficult to achieve, particularly in the big company, but if we want heterogeneous leadership resources to meet the unpredictable needs of the future we certainly will not get them by subjecting all our managerial trainees to the same treatment.

Moreover, this process of developing heterogeneous resources must be continuous; it is never completed. Few human beings ever realize all of their potentialities for growth, even though some may reach a practical limit with respect to certain capacities. Each individual is unique, and it is this uniqueness we will constantly encourage and nourish if we are truly concerned to develop leaders for the industry of tomorrow.

Fourth, the promotion policies of the company should be so administered that these heterogeneous resources are actually considered when openings occur. There is little value in developing a wide range of talent if only a small and possibly limited segment of it constitutes the field of candidates when a particular position is being filled.

In view of the selective operation of situational variables referred to above, there may be legitimate questions concerning the value of an *exclusive* policy of "promotion from within." It is conceivable that in a large and reasonably decentralized company sufficient heterogeneity can be maintained by transfers of managerial talent between divisions, but it is probable that fairly strenuous efforts will be required to offset the normal tendency to create and maintain a "type," a homogeneous pattern of leadership within a given organization. Without such efforts, competent individuals who do not "fit the pattern" are likely to be passed over or to leave because their talents are not rewarded. Many industrial organizations, for example, would not easily tolerate the strong individualism of a young Charles Kettering today.

People Come First

Finally, if leadership is a function—a complex relation between leader and situation—we ought to be clear that every promising recruit is *not* a potential member of top management. Some people in some companies will become outstanding leaders as foremen, or as plant superintendents, or as professional specialists. Many of these would not be effective leaders in top management positions, at least under the circumstances prevailing in the company.

If we take seriously the implications of the research findings in this field, we will place high value on such people. We will seek to enable them to develop to the fullest their potentialities in the role they can fill best. And we will find ways to reward them that will persuade them that we consider outstanding leadership at any level to be a precious thing.

PART THREE

■

UNION-
MANAGEMENT
RELATIONS

7

Union - Management Cooperation:
A Psychological Analysis

SINCE THE CAMPAIGN of the War Production Board [in 1941] many plants throughout the country have been experimenting with labor-management production-drive committees. The results achieved have varied tremendously. Some of these committees have been dismal failures. Many have been mildly successful. A few have been so successful that the participants themselves have been startled.

The idea that cooperation between management and union might be a powerful force to increase productive efficiency is not a new one. It has been the subject of experimentation for many years in a few industries, notably the railroads, certain branches of the men's clothing and the needle trades, and, more recently, steel.[1] However, this

Written in collaboration with Irving Knickerbocker, this article appeared in *Personnel*, 1942, *19*, No. 3, 520–539.
[1] Cf. S. H. Slichter, *Union Policies and Industrial Management.* Washington, D.C.: The Brookings Institution, 1941, Chaps. 14–19; and C. S. Golden and H. J. Ruttenberg, *The Dynamics of Industrial Democracy.* New York: Harper and Brothers, 1942, Chaps. 8 and 9.

campaign of the War Production Board has been the first attempt to promote such cooperation on a large scale.

The literature contains a number of case studies of union-management cooperation as well as many partisan arguments on the subject,[2] but there have been few attempts to analyze union-management cooperation from a psychological point of view. Nevertheless, cooperation is a relationship between people. It is, therefore, a psychological phenomenon. The purpose of this article is to present an analysis in terms of some of the important psychological factors that influence the success or failure of cooperation between management and union.

The emphasis in this analysis will be upon the relationship between management and union *within* the company. We shall be concerned with the thinking and behavior of workers, union leaders, and management in an industrial organization. We shall discuss attitudes, points of view, personality traits, and habits of thought and action as important psychological factors determining the nature of the relationship.

Without in any sense denying their importance, we shall ignore external, social, and economic factors such as the impact of the business cycle. Although the details of the relationships will undoubtedly differ as these external factors change, it is nevertheless true that all forms of union-management relations are to be found under almost any given set of external circumstances. This is an analysis of the psychological determinants of labor-management relations *within* the plant.

[2] For references, cf. *Union-Management Cooperation with Special Reference to the War Production Drive*. Industrial Relations Section, Princeton University, Princeton, N.J., May 1942.

Union-Management Relations as a Process of Psychological Growth

It has frequently been noted that union-management relations follow a fairly typical course of historical change. When a union is first organized in a plant, the relationship is likely to involve a high degree of suspicion and conflict. Usually this "fighting stage" gradually disappears and is followed by a relatively neutral stage characterized by a decrease of suspicion, a growth in mutual understanding, and in general a mildly friendly atmosphere. This is the stage of successful collective bargaining. Where circumstances have been favorable, a third stage in union-management relations emerges. This is a stage in which suspicion and conflict have disappeared, and in which the atmosphere is one not alone of acceptance but of constructive joint efforts to solve common problems. The term *union-management cooperation* has been applied to this third stage of the historical process.

This transition from stage to stage becomes more meaningful if it is viewed not merely as a process of historical change, but as a process of psychological growth and development similar to that experienced by the individual as he passes from infancy through childhood and adolescence to maturity. The transition becomes even more meaningful if the emphasis is laid on the emotional aspects of the developmental process rather than on the intellectual aspects alone.

There are four important characteristics of psychological growth that apply equally to the individual and to union-management relations. In the first place, psychological growth is a slow and arduous process. It involves a myriad of small changes in thinking and behavior which normally occur imperceptibly day by day. Although the rate of growth may vary somewhat, depending upon circumstances, sudden jumps occur rarely and then only as a consequence of rather severe crises. Thus, some cooperative plans have emerged suddenly as a result of the very real threat of the complete bankruptcy of the company. This is not normal growth, but an abnormal "spurt" brought about by a crisis.

In the second place, psychological growth is not an all-or-nothing process. Even the emotionally mature adult retains some childish habits. On the other hand, the child can in some ways be startlingly mature. The same thing is true of union-management relations. The growth process is uneven; maturity is achieved in one small way today and in another tomorrow. Many "childish" habits and ways of thinking are retained long after their usefulness has apparently disappeared. The differences between one stage of union-management relations and another can be viewed only in the over-all sense. Detailed analysis reveals elements of every stage at any given time. Each individual participant possesses some habits and attitudes that are childish and others that are mature, and the interacting individuals differ among themselves in their over-all maturity.

The third characteristic of growth is that it may be arrested at any stage. Just as some individuals of forty are still at an adolescent level of emotional development, so do some union-management relationships remain in the fighting stage for long periods of time. This characteristic of being arrested in the course of development is so common that real emotional maturity is rare among individuals. Likewise genuine cooperation between union and management is rare. When one recognizes how complex are the necessary emotional adjustments between individuals and groups in union-management relations, it is not surprising that only a small proportion of union-management combinations have succeeded in reaching a fair degree of maturity.

Finally, psychological growth, unlike physical growth, is a two-way process. Retrogression is not at all unusual. Occasionally, in a critical situation, mature habits and ways of thinking that have been acquired painfully and slowly will suddenly disappear, to be supplanted by childish ones that have been presumed to be long since dead. In an extreme sense this phenomenon may be observed when civilized people become barbarians under the stress of strong emotions (for example, in a lynching mob). The same phenomenon may be observed in a milder form when, in a cooperative meeting between union and management, someone inadvertently brings up a point that strikes at the heart of an emotional "blind spot" of one or more of the participants. Sometimes the results of the retrogression last not for minutes or hours but for months or even years.

In the end, the psychological growth of union-management relations is no more than the growth of the participating individuals. The situation in any given organization is exceedingly complex because of the varying extent to which one individual or another dominates the picture, and because a number of different individuals are participating in the relationship.

The process of psychological growth in labor-management relations takes place through the interaction of the participants. The interaction occurs in face-to-face meetings between representatives of the two groups, and in the day-to-day contacts between individuals on the job. A change in management's ways of acting or thinking influences the union, and results in a change (not necessarily the same one, to be sure) on the part of the union. This alteration in the union's thought or action in turn reacts upon management, and through the circular interaction the relationship develops.

In the past, there was very little interaction, because management dominated the relationship almost completely. During the past decade, the development of the union movement has changed the picture from one of *action* by management on the workers to one of *interaction* between them. Interaction is the means by which the relationship grows.

The Difference between Collective Bargaining and Cooperation

The use of two different terms may imply mutually exclusive phenomena, but in this case that is not intended. Collective bargaining and cooperation are terms referring to overlapping stages of development in union-management relations. Just as a relatively mature adolescent may be more like an adult than like the average adolescent, so may collective bargaining in a mature relationship resemble cooperation more than it resembles typical collective bargaining. In the discussion that follows, we shall describe an arbitrarily selected point in each of two wide ranges of phenomena. Our descriptions are intended to throw into relief the differences between the two processes, and therefore the selected points are well separated. Many individual instances of collective bargaining or cooperation are more or less mature than those that would be fitted exactly by our definitions.

Collective bargaining is essentially a competitive process. It arose historically by carrying over to the relationship between union and management certain practices that were at one time habitual in the relationship between competing firms. The bargainer tries to outguess the other fellow, to hide his own motives, to play up the concessions he grants his opponent, and to play down those he receives. The process is reasonably well characterized by the metaphor of "playing one's cards close to the chest."

Genuine cooperation, on the other hand, is a shared effort on the part of individuals or groups to achieve jointly desired goals. It is not a bargaining process, even though it may develop from bargaining practices. Effective cooperation can occur only when the "cards are face up on the table." Regardless of appearances and "stage dressing," real collective bargaining is essentially characterized by conflict, cooperation by mutual aid.

We are not attempting to criticize collective bargaining or to praise cooperation. Both procedures have important roles in union-management relations. Collective bargaining does not disappear when cooperation emerges. There are some problems, notably wage negotiation, that are likely to remain matters for collective bargaining regardless of the degree of cooperation that exists between a union and management.

There is nevertheless some shift as the developmental process takes place. Some of the things that were originally dealt with through collective bargaining come in time to be dealt with cooperatively. For example, a great many grievances come to be handled in time by cooperative means. As the union and management deal with each other, and as mutual trust and confidence begin to develop, there comes a gradual recognition that the real aim of a grievance procedure is the solution of common problems to the equal satisfaction of all concerned. This recognition leads to a tendency to look behind the immediate, apparently conflicting demands presented with any particular grievance to the really basic desires that are present but unexpressed. In many cases the basic desires of the two parties are found not to be incompatible.[3] When this occurs, the settling of a grievance becomes a cooperative procedure in which both sides attempt to find a solution equally satisfying to both. To the extent that this happens, the grievance procedure becomes a cooperative process rather than one of collective bargaining. There are some grievances, of course, that involve a genuine conflict of interest or desire, and these cannot be handled cooperatively.

It is perfectly possible for union and management to cooperate on some things and to compete on others. What is not possible is for them to compete and to cooperate at once on the same problem. Matters for collective bargaining (involving conflict) cannot at one and the same time be matters for cooperation (involving mutual aid). This point is fundamental, and must be realized by both parties before genuine cooperation becomes possible. It is for this reason that companies setting up joint production-drive committees were urged by the War Production Board not to permit matters connected with collective bargaining to be discussed in the meetings of the production committees.

Recently a member of management in a discussion with union leaders raised a question that is pertinent here. He said to the union leaders: "When you fellows go on to the point where you have organized practically all of industry, and when you have gotten practically all you can get from management without forcing it into bankruptcy, what then?" This question points to the fundamental distinction between collective bargaining and cooperation. If the returns from a business enterprise are considered to be a pie, there are two ways for the union to get more pie. One way is to fight for as big a piece as can be obtained. That is col-

[3] Cf. Mary Follett, *Creative Experience*. New York: Longmans, Green, 1924.

lective bargaining. If the union has gotten as big a piece as possible by this means, there remains another way: To strive to increase the size of the pie so that there will be more for everyone who partakes of it. The concept of union-management cooperation springs from the latter point of view.

There is one more point to be considered in connection with the distinction between collective bargaining and co-operation. We have already indicated that some problems are likely to remain matters of collective bargaining indefinitely. What, then, are the problems that lend themselves most readily to cooperative effort? One thinks first of the problems of productive efficiency. Through cooperative effort it is possible to increase output and reduce waste, thus increasing the size of the pie.

Many companies have experimented with cooperative procedures for dealing with other problems. For example, although the establishment of the general level of wages is accomplished through collective bargaining, problems connected with the internal wage structure may be handled with considerable success on a cooperative basis. Job evaluation plans are rather widely administered today on a joint basis.[4] A few firms have had some success in the joint administration of wage incentive systems.[5] Many problems connected with the formulation of a general labor policy, such as would be printed in a booklet or new employees, can be successfully handled cooperatively.[6] As suggested above, the grievance procedure is in part amenable to a cooperative approach. There have even been instances where the union has

[4] Cf. H. B. Bergen, "Union Participation in Job Evaluation." *Personnel*, 1942, *18*, No. 5, 261–268.
[5] The Murray Corporation, Detroit, is an outstanding example.
[6] D. D. Decker, "A Practical Supervisory Training Program." *Personnel*, 1939, *16*, No. 2, 62–68.

cooperated with the company on problems connected with merchandising and selling.[7]

Union-management cooperation may encompass a variety of phenomena. It begins to appear in rudimentary form during the neutral, or collective bargaining, stage of the relationship. Its further development is often unnecessarily delayed because of a failure of the participants to recognize clearly the essential differences between collective bargaining and cooperation.

Basic Differences in Union and Management Organization

We have pointed out that growth in union-management relations takes place through the medium of the interaction of representatives of the two groups. Certain basic differences between the management organization and the union organization materially affect the nature of the interaction that takes place and thus influence the growth of union-management relations. The most important difference, and the only one that we shall discuss, is in the way in which authority and responsibility are handled by the management organization and the union organization.

Industrial management is so organized that control is from the top down, with authority and responsibility delegated by the few to the many. Those at the top who have final authority are presumably the most capable and the most skilled of the whole management group.

The control by those at the top is exerted over the man-

[7] Jules Hochman, *Industry Planning Through Collective Bargaining*. A program for modernizing the New York Dress Industry, as presented in conference with employers on behalf of the Joint Board of the Dressmakers' Union. International Ladies' Garment Workers Union, New York, 1941.

agement organization through the formulation of a policy that sets limits within which action may be taken by the rest of the group. This policy is usually a fairly general one and emphasizes long-range achievements. It may be written down, or it may exist only in the minds of those at the top. It may be implemented by few or many rules and regulations.

Top management policy is aimed at the promotion of a profitable enterprise.[8] This is essentially the reason for the existence of the management organization. In promoting a profitable enterprise, management is likely to stress in its policy the necessity for freedom of action, and to feel that, without it, control of the business (purchasing, manufacturing, sales) is lost. Restrictions are placed upon the authority and responsibility of subordinates so that they will not through their actions interfere with top management's control.

Top management also exerts a fundamental control upon the rest of the management organization through its methods of selecting and training subordinates. A certain degree of conformity with top management policy is required of all subordinates. Those who do not conform are dropped from the organization. A conscious control is exerted in this manner. However, men are selected as a result of unconscious influences that are even more important. A member of management chooses his subordinates not only to fill the logical requirements of his organization, but also to satisfy certain unconscious demands of his own personality. A commonly recognized example is the executive who surrounds himself with "yes men."

Finally, top management exerts control by issuing orders.

---

[8] There are, of course, top managements whose policies are aimed actually at the achievement of purely personal goals (money, power, etc.). These are not under discussion in the present article.

These may be broad or specific; they may be called by a variety of names, but essentially they are orders that must be followed within certain limits of tolerance by subordinates within the organization. Even the most liberal top management, using the consultative methods that are popular today, retains a veto power over the actions and decisions of its subordinates.

In union organizations, on the other hand, control is ultimately from the bottom upward, with authority and responsibility delegated by the many to the few.[9] The many who control are usually less skilled and less capable than the leaders whom they control.

The aims of the rank and file are likely to be relatively opportunistic and short-range. Further, they are likely to be very specific rather than general in nature: get this wage increase, settle that grievance to our satisfaction, prevent management from carrying out this course of action, etc.

In the early stages of union-management relations, one of the chief aims of the union membership may be revenge.[10] This depends, of course, upon the past behavior of management. Where this desire for revenge exists, it is usually found that the provision of an opportunity for the open expression of accumulated dissatisfactions removes the necessity for other forms of revengeful behavior. When management has a sincere desire to eliminate past sources of frustration of its workers, there is little need to fear a long continuance of the revenge theme.

The union membership will also try to obtain specific improvements in working conditions and changes in procedural

---

[9] Although it is true that there are many "boss-ridden" unions, these, like the racketeer managements mentioned in the previous footnote, are arbitrarily eliminated from this discussion. Even among boss-ridden *international* unions there are many "boss-free" union *locals*.

[10] Cf. Golden and Ruttenberg, *op. cit.*, Chap. I, especially pp. 15, 16.

rules such as those of promotion and transfer. Finally, it will be their aim to obtain more money. The important needs for social recognition, security, and recognition of personal worth are difficult for the worker to put into words. The demand for money is tangible. It is therefore an excellent medium for the expression of these needs.

Other aims of a different nature will emerge only after a slow educational process by which first the leaders and then the membership of the union have been brought to the point of thinking in long-range terms.

The authority of the union membership is exerted ultimately through their elected leaders. There is a vast difference between the elective process and the carefully controlled selective and training processes utilized by top management. In addition, at least during the early period of the union's existence, the union demands a greater conformity from its leaders than does management from its subordinates.

Members of management sometimes fail to recognize the consequences of these facts about the union organization. They display a kind of impatience that suggests that they expect to deal with the union in the same way that they would deal with the management of another firm. However, in the early stages of union-management relations, union leaders are specifically instructed delegates. They come to management with explicit instructions to obtain certain definite things. They are not carrying on negotiations within the framework of a policy, expressed or unexpressed.

As time passes and the union attains a greater stability and security, the control over its leaders is somewhat looser. Management's education of the union leaders begins to bear fruit. They can begin to operate within the framework of a policy. Nevertheless, because a union local is basically a democratic organization, union leaders must constantly check the opinions of their constituents to see whether the decisions they are reaching in their negotiations with management are consistent with the aims of the membership. The rank and file always lag behind their leaders in understanding and in willingness to accept broad policies and long-range aims.[11]

There is sometimes an interesting consequence of this "lag." A management that has been dealing with union leaders who have developed and broadened remarkably in perspective may be surprised to find them replaced at election time by a group of suspicious and antagonistic "fighters." What has happened is this: the old leaders, effectively educated by management, have failed in turn to educate the membership of the union, and the "lag" has become too great. *From the point of view of the members*, the leaders have "sold out" to management. They are suspicious not only of their leaders but of the management that has "betrayed" them, and they proceed to elect a new leadership that will "show management where to get off."

Union leaders are not alone in being restricted by the attitudes and capacities of their followers. Management is also restricted to some extent by the capacities and attitudes of its subordinates. Many firms have faced a real problem in the re-education of a group of "unenlightened" old line foremen after a union has been organized in the plant. After facing this problem, management will have a much clearer conception of what a union is up against.

[11] Management's employment policies will, in the long run, materially affect the growth of union-management relations by determining the quality of workers that are employed. Marginal firms, hiring from the lower fringes of the labor market, cannot expect the education of the rank and file of the membership to proceed as rapidly as does that of firms that select their workers from the "cream of the crop."

We have indicated certain differences in the handling of authority and responsibility by the management organization and the union organization. These differences materially affect the nature of the interaction between management representatives and union representatives. All the discussion that follows must be seen against this background of the difference in nature of the two organizations. The requirements for effective cooperation would be entirely different if the management organization and the union organization handled authority and responsibility in identical ways.

The Influence of the Personalities of Management

It is obvious that the nature of the interaction between management and union will be influenced by the personalities of the participants.[12] Considering management first, we shall discuss one broad characteristic of personality that has a vital influence upon the rate of growth of union-management relations.

The growth will be exceedingly slow and may cease altogether at an early stage of development, unless the key members of management who regularly deal with the union have a genuine, secure confidence in themselves and in their ability to perform the functions of management.

This self-confidence will reflect itself in a variety of ways. The men who possess it are quietly sure of themselves. They know (but they probably do not say so) that whatever

[12] This is a complex subject. There are a great many ways in which the personalities of the participants influence union-management relations. Within the scope of this paper we can present only a grossly oversimplified discussion of one or two aspects of the problem. For a more detailed discussion of the influences of personality on social interaction, see, for example: A. H. Maslow, and B. Mittelmann, *Principles of Abnormal Psychology*. New York: Harper and Brothers, 1941, esp. Chaps. 4, 14–16.

happens they will be able to land on their feet. They are able to take criticism, even from their inferiors. They are tolerant—able to see and to face the limitations placed upon union leaders by the nature of the union organization. Since they have a secure confidence in themselves, they can face critical problems in human relations objectively. Their own inferiorities do not become involved in the situation. Consequently, they are able to take a long-range view of the union-management relationship, and their decisions will stand the test of time.

This basic self-confidence is not so common as might be supposed. Many able managers lack it. Many who are not so able reveal its absence by an overbearing manner.

A lack of self-confidence among the key members of management retards union-management cooperation by slowing up the growth of the relationship in several important ways. The member of management who is lacking in self-confidence cannot treat union representatives as equals. The relationship will be that of the master accepting somewhat warily the help of the slave, with fear and trembling lest the slave overpower him and assume the role of master. Under such conditions the growth process is fixated at a relatively early stage, because genuine cooperation involves at least a measure of equality between the participants.

The individual who lacks self-confidence fears and suspects those with whom he deals, particularly if they are somewhat antagonistic and aggressive. As a result of this fear and suspicion, he will be unwilling to take the *necessary* chances involved in the early stages of union-management cooperation. It is inevitable that the first attempt at cooperation will be harried by hang-overs of past competitive habits. Particularly when the past experience of both parties has involved a fair amount of conflict, they are likely to "stub their toes" frequently when they begin to attempt to co-operate. It requires real confidence to accept these slips and to go on without the feeling that there has been a "dirty deal."

In summary, then, a vital factor influencing the growth of industrial relations will be the presence or absence of a genuine, secure confidence on the part of the key members of management who deal with the union.[13] If this is absent, union-management relations are likely to be arrested at an early stage of the process. Only in the presence of this factor will management have the courage to take the inevitable risks involved in making a transition from the neutral to the cooperative stage of union-management relations.

The Influence of the Personalities of Union Leaders

The man who has rebelled violently against authority is rarely tolerated in management. He is, however, frequently found among those union leaders who are in power during the fighting stage of union-management relations. He is elected to his office because he possesses exactly the characteristics that the new and insecure union requires if it is to achieve the things its members desire of it at that time. His first appearance across the table from management may cause a good deal of consternation. Such a man is likely to

[13] It may appear that we are more tolerant of weaknesses in unions than in management. We are, and for a definite reason: The weaknesses of the union movement have been amply criticized in the press, in literature, and from the lecture platform. Constructive criticism of management is far less frequent. The union movement today is a powerful force. We believe that management has much to gain by understanding it, and by learning how to live with it. Hence our emphasis on the ways in which management can change in order to influence the growth of the relationship.

be resentful toward management and completely unwilling to bury the past in order to build a new relationship. Consequently, the growth of industrial relations is arrested so long as he is in power.

In the normal course of events, however, the union achieves some of its purposes, and with this achievement comes a measure of security. When this happens, there is likely to be a change in union leadership. Men get tired of fighting (particularly when it is unnecessary), of fiery oratory, of being whipped into a frenzy at every union meeting. They want someone who will lead them and protect their interests without creating such a fuss about it. They are ready to elect to office intelligent leaders who are quietly confident and who possess skill in dealing with men. It is not until such men are elected to office by the union that the transition to later stages of union-management relations becomes possible.

The Quality of Foremanship

Interaction between management and union occurs chiefly in two ways: (1) through meetings between middle or top management and union leaders, and (2) through the daily contact between foreman and union members. The union *leader* acquires an understanding of management's problems, learns the why and the wherefore of company policy, and forms his opinions of "the Company" by means of his contact with the higher levels of management. The union *member* acquires his understanding and forms his opinions about "the Company" (1) from what he is told by the leaders of his union, and (2) from his experience with his foreman. When there are discrepancies between (1) and (2), the union member (like most of us) accepts the evidence of experience. As a result, discrepancies between the "teachings" of top management and those of the foremen will either forestall management's attempts to broaden and develop the union leaders, or will undermine the union leadership by widening the gap between leaders and members.

It is obvious, therefore, that the foreman's methods of handling his men, his attitudes, and his personality are important factors influencing the growth of union-management relations.[14] The most progressive and well-intentioned top management may find that its efforts to promote better relations are not achieving the desired results because the foremen resent the union and reveal their resentment in their treatment of the workers. The situation is further aggravated if management (as is often the case) fails to recognize the effect of the behavior of the foremen upon the workers. Failing to perceive the real cause, top management may feel that the union members are unreasonable and recalcitrant. Then the fighting stage of the relationship may be prolonged until the union educates the foremen or succeeds in "running out" the worst of them.

Thus the poor foreman may prevent the execution of the most carefully laid plans for improving union-management relations. He may even provide the reason for the belief that better relations are impossible. Too often he does both, and management—unaware of the real circumstances—unjustly accuses the union of bad faith.

The good foreman, on the other hand, provides a daily proof of management's real intentions. From his behavior the union members may obtain the substantiating evidence that their leaders need to sell them an enlightened, long-range program.

It is apparent, then, that the growth of union-management relations is vitally dependent upon the quality of men se-

[14] Cf. R. B. Hersey, "Labor Relations of 1941: Cooperation vs. Dictation." *Personnel,* 1941, *17,* No. 4, 270–288.

lected to be foremen, upon their training, and upon the degree to which they are made an integral part of management. Cooperation between management and union cannot occur until there is cooperation within the ranks of management.

A Recognition of the Ability of the Average Worker

The union and the management must each expect the other to contribute something worth while to the solution of their joint problems if there is to be any point in cooperating. This means that each group must recognize in the other an ability that, if utilized, will contribute importantly to their cooperative effort.

Workers in general respect management's ability, even though they may not respect management's philosophy and motives. Management, on the other hand, has a tendency to underestimate those abilities of workers that may be utilized for cooperative efforts. Aware of the long period of apprenticeship they themselves have served, many members of management are likely to feel that it is absurd to assume that workers could be of material help in promoting more efficient production. So long as the worker is regarded as a mere "quantum of labor," the idea of union-management cooperation is preposterous.

This underevaluation of the worker's potential contribution is especially prevalent where management lacks real self-confidence. When an individual lacks confidence in his own ability, he does not readily recognize it in others. He is likely to protect his opinion of himself by underestimating the ability of the other fellow, particularly if the other fellow occupies a lower position on the social scale.

The abilities of the worker that may be tapped for the cooperative effort differ from those of management. That is the main reason why they are valuable. Management typically has a generalized knowledge of engineering principles and of the production problems and processes in the plant. The worker, on the other hand, has a highly specific knowledge, drawn from his intimate daily contact with the process on which he is working and the machine he operates. As a result, he can often assist management materially in discovering ways of improving the process, of reducing waste, of increasing the efficiency of a machine.

Because he is quite unfettered by a knowledge of the principles of physics, chemistry, and engineering, he is frequently able to view the process on which he is working with a perspective that would be impossible for management. A great many important contributions in science and engineering have come about because the inventor was able to take an absolutely fresh slant on the problem. This, above all else, the worker can do. Out of his fresh perspective sometimes emerge suggestions and ideas which, although they may appear initially to be foolish, have real merit. The literature of union-management cooperation contains example after example of suggestions submitted by workers that have proved practical after management has overcome its initial skepticism sufficiently to experiment with them.[15]

Because the worker is likely to be overawed by management's knowledge and ability, he is likely to keep his mouth shut for fear of criticism and ridicule. Management must have a genuine and evident respect for his ability before he will feel free to express himself.

We are not suggesting that management must be prepared

[15] Cf. Golden and Ruttenberg, *op. cit.*, Chaps. 8 and 9.

to put into practice every idea suggested by its workers if cooperation is to be effective. We are suggesting that the cooperation will be fruitless unless management has learned to deal with these suggestions in a way that does not injure the worker's rather shaky belief in his own ability along these lines. Also, management must be flexible enough intellectually to recognize potential merit in a fresh point of view, and to experiment with ideas that may seem revolutionary in the light of accepted engineering principles. The history of science is full of examples of great discoveries that were ridiculed merely because they were somewhat unusual.

The member of management who lacks faith in the worker's ability will demonstrate it readily in his reaction to the idea of union-management cooperation. He will feel and say that it is a waste of time. Although he will not be so likely to say it, he will also feel that it is insulting to him to have to accept the help of workers in solving his problems. He believes that he is on top of the heap because of his own ability, and that workers are on the bottom because they lack it.

The existence of the ability denied the worker by management is often demonstrated when it is utilized to defeat management's purposes. It is the boast of many workers that they can "beat" any incentive system that management can devise, and the evidence tends to support this contention. The longer union-management relations remain in the fighting stage, the more strongly are union members motivated to utilize their abilities in order to outsmart management. It is only when the relationship has gone beyond the neutral stage that these abilities can be harnessed for the solution of common problems.

This respect for the ability of the worker has a corollary: a realization of the potentialities of the worker for learning.

Workers are likely to be humble concerning their own potentialities for development and learning, but they are ordinarily eager to learn if properly motivated. The fruits of union-management cooperation will not be realized unless management takes advantage of these potentialities.

A Willingness to Share Equitably the Gains from Cooperation

Neither management nor union will ever seriously consider the possibility of cooperation unless they expect to gain from it. It is probably unwise to depend too much on the purely philanthropic motives of man. Even the patriotic motives appealed to by the War Production Board in its campaign for production-drive committees are likely to operate only to the extent that management and workers alike view the war as something very close to home. When the present crisis really is a crisis in their eyes—when they honestly believe that their own efforts can help to prevent a catastrophe —only then will this appeal be an effective one in promoting their joint efforts to cooperate. As of August 1942, one may be permitted to doubt whether this kind of motivation is as yet very widespread.

There are a number of possible gains from union-management cooperation that the worker will recognize as important to *him*. The motives involved can be harnessed to the cooperative effort, however, only if there is a genuine willingness to share equitably the resulting gains.

The first of these gains is the economic one. There is plenty of evidence to suggest that the economic gains can be sizable, but there is not so much evidence of a willingness on management's part to share them equitably. Many suggestion schemes have been set up as a means of stimulating the worker's ideas for the promotion of greater productive efficiency. Even the more liberal of these plans seldom grant the worker an equitable share in the results obtained from his suggestions. Many of them have a top award of $50 or $100, although savings effected through the suggestions submitted sometimes total thousands of dollars per year.

The traditional American philosophy has been individualistic. Consequently, it has been natural for management to seek ways of motivating individuals to be more productive, and to reward the individual for his efforts. During the past decade, however, there has been an increasing emphasis on collective goals. Social security, "share-the-work" plans, union organization, wage and hour legislation—all are *group* rather than individual phenomena. It is actually just as possible to harness motives to group effort as it is to individual effort,[16] although we have only recently begun to recognize the fact in industry.

Union-management cooperation is a group effort. Although effective cooperation is unlikely if the contributions of the individual to the collective effort are ignored entirely, the economic gains can best be shared on a group basis. The economic gains of cooperation do not go to individual members of management. There is no reason for them to go to individual members of the union. Some of the other gains can be shared in a way that rewards the contributions of the individual.

There is a growing realization today that the possibility of economic gain is only one of many reasons that keep the worker (as well as management) on the job. A second

[16] The recent writings of the social anthropologists provide ample evidence. Cf., for example, Margaret Mead, *Cooperation and Competition Among Primitive Peoples*. New York: McGraw-Hill Book Company, 1937.

highly important motive is the desire for prestige and social recognition. Properly handled, this motive becomes a powerful asset to union-management cooperation. The efforts of both the individual and the group may be rewarded by proper recognition.

Investigators of the War Production Board, reporting on the experiences of companies that have installed production-drive committees, point out that one of the major obstacles to successful cooperation has been the unwillingness of management to give the union proper credit for its contribution to the joint effort. There is something ironic in the fact that management, traditionally motivated *solely* by the desire for profits, is sometimes loath to share prestige with its own workers. Nevertheless, this unwillingness on the part of management has proved a stumbling block to successful cooperation many times in the past.

Once more, we refer to the factor of management's confidence in its own ability, which was discussed above. The member of management who is not genuinely confident of himself feels that he loses face when his workers gain prestige for having contributed importantly to an increase in productive efficiency. He feels that, since the management of the productive processes is his concern and responsibility, any improvement in them that he has not instituted is essentially a criticism of his own skill. Naturally, then, he is unwilling to see others obtain praise, since he regards that praise as criticism of himself.

One of the outstanding examples of union-management cooperation in the country has been plagued recently by this bugaboo. The remarkable success of this venture has resulted in considerable publicity. Because of the man-bites-dog feature of the situation, the publicity has stressed the contributions of the union to the cooperative effort. In the recent past, management has begun to play down the contributions of the union when discussing the situation with visitors. In this particular instance the problem is probably not a serious one, because the relationship between management and union has become so mature that the issue will undoubtedly be discussed openly and cleared up by both sides before it becomes critical. The example is significant because it illustrates the fact that, even though the economic issue is settled, the problem of sharing the further results of cooperation (prestige in this case) can be a real one, even though union-management relations have reached a remarkable degree of maturity. It is likely to be a much more critical problem in the early stages of cooperation.

The gains from union-management cooperation can be shared with the workers in another important way: in terms of job security. When the Baltimore and Ohio railroad began union-management cooperation back in 1923, the guarantee by the company that induced the union to try out the plan was one of job security. Certainly, if cooperation is effective, it will strengthen the position of the company competitively and to that extent make possible a greater stabilization of employment and greater guarantees of job security. With the experiences of the past decade still fresh in their minds, this is a matter of considerable importance to workers.

Some well-known instances of union-management cooperation in the steel industry and in the needle trades were begun as a last resort in companies that were about to go out of existence because of financial insecurity. Job security was obviously a fundamental motive in such cases. It has been suggested by some critics that effective union-management cooperation can occur only under such extreme circumstances. It is more probable that these cases represent examples of a sudden maturing of union-management relations brought about by the necessity for surviving a real crisis. The growth process was speeded up materially in these instances. If the course of development had been normal, the stage of union-management cooperation might well have been delayed for several years.

There are other potential gains from union-management cooperation that are somewhat intangible. Chief among these is the interest in the "game" of running the company successfully. There is little doubt that this is a basic motive of management. It can be shared with workers. When it is shared, some of the workers at least will begin to display the same loyalty to the company that is expected of management. The sharing of this interest inevitably narrows the gap between management and union.

Economic gains, prestige, increased job security, and interest in "the game" are all potential consequences of union-management cooperation. Unless there is a genuine willingness to share the results equitably, there will be not only a lack of motivation for the cooperative effort but a real dissatisfaction with the whole relationship. Without a plan for the equitable sharing of results, the idea of cooperation will probably be viewed as an attempt on management's part to bring about a speed-up. The consequence of such suspicion is not cooperation but its antithesis.

Union Security

When a union is fighting with management for its existence, union-management cooperation is impossible. Its leaders are motivated primarily to get more and more from management through collective bargaining so that they will remain in office and the workers will remain in the union. When the

union has achieved some form of security (e.g., a mainte-
nance-of-membership clause, a union shop, or a closed shop),
its leaders will no longer have to weigh every move in terms
of what their constituents will have to say about it. They
can weigh the problems they discuss with management in
terms of their real merit rather than in terms of their political
significance for the union membership. They can count on
time in which to educate their followers and in which to
demonstrate the value of long-range rather than short-range
goals.

This issue is a difficult one to discuss, because the arguments that are usually advanced contain far more heat than
light.[17] Regardless of the merits of the case, there is very
little doubt that some form of union security is essential if
union-management relations are to develop to full maturity.
It may well be that a new formula for union security will
be discovered which will be superior to any of those commonly used today. One formula that seems to have been almost entirely ignored is to share the gains of union-management cooperation between the groups that are cooperating,
namely, the management (or the owners) and the membership of the union. There is thus provided a genuine
motivation for joining the union, and the problems of
coercion and freedom of contract are not involved.[18] Union
members may be unwilling to expend the effort involved in
union-management cooperation if the fruits are to be shared
alike with members and nonmembers.

In general it may be pointed out that union security is
normally an issue only during the early stages of the growth

[17] For a well-documented, objective analysis of the issue, cf. J. L. Toner,
The Closed Shop. Washington, D.C.: American Council on Public Affairs,
1942.

[18] The fact that management is ordinarily unfavorably disposed toward
this arrangement indicates that the reasons usually advanced against the
union shop are not the basic ones.

of union-management relations. When these relations have reached the stage where cooperation is being seriously considered, and where a fair proportion of the factors mentioned above are present, the question of union security is likely to be settled with very little argument.

Mutual Understanding

If the reader will look back over the whole list of factors we have discussed, it will be apparent to him that one that has not yet been mentioned specifically runs through all of them as a common thread. This factor is a genuine mutual understanding on the part of the participants in the union-management relationship. Only when this understanding is present is it possible for growth to occur.

Unless management understands the problems of the union leaders that arise as a result of the nature of a union organization, the behavior of the leaders will be viewed with suspicion and sometimes even contempt. Unless the union leaders can acquire a genuine understanding of the authoritative relationships of management and their consequences, they will remain suspicious and antagonistic.

Unless management understands the worker's desires for security, social satisfactions, prestige, and the recognition of personal worth, union-management cooperation will appear to be a utopian idea entirely outside the realm of practicality.

On the other hand, unless the union can acquire a genuine understanding of management's desire for a productive enterprise, many of management's suggestions for improving efficiency and reducing waste will be viewed with suspicion. Unless the union members can acquire an understanding of cost reduction through a knowledge of the problems of their company, there is little point in cooperative effort to improve productive efficiency.

This mutual understanding, which is so essential to the development of labor-management relations, is not a mere intellectual phenomenon. If someone says to you, "I want to explain how this machine works," and then proceeds to show you blueprints and demonstrations of the operations of the machine in question, you will end (if he is competent) with an "understanding" of what he is talking about.

On the other hand, suppose someone says to you, "I want you to understand how I felt when I asked the boss for a raise the other day," and then goes on to describe his feelings as he approached the boss, his reaction when he discovered that the boss was in a bad temper because he had just lost a large order to his chief competitor, and his crushing disappointment when the request for a raise was indignantly refused. Whether or not you "understand" in this case depends not upon a mere knowledge of the facts but upon your ability to put yourself into the other fellow's shoes emotionally. This ability to put yourself in the place of the other fellow and to feel as he does is an important means by which tolerance and trust are developed in people who deal with each other day by day.

Union-management meetings are often carried on in an atmosphere of "being logical" or "sticking to the hard facts." When this atmosphere exists, a barrier is raised against the expression of feelings and emotions. The man who insists on logic and facts will almost certainly fail to get "out on the table" the nonlogical opinions and feelings that are important to real understanding. Cooperation under these circumstances is an impossibility.

We have aimed high in this discussion, but we do not believe we have been unrealistic. None of these requirements for union-management cooperation are impractical, although some of them may be difficult to achieve in particular situations at particular times. Instances of really successful cooperation are indeed rare, partly because union-management relations in this country are still generally in the early stages of growth, and partly because most people do not realize the requirements for genuine cooperation. The existence of even a few remarkably mature relationships gives the lie to those who insist that union-management cooperation is but an idealist's pipedream.

There are many union-management combinations that are today, after a normal healthy growth, enjoying a collective bargaining relationship that they would have thought fantastic a few years ago. If they have the patience to accept the inevitable slowness and unevenness of psychological growth, if each side has enough self-confidence to permit a belief in the ability and honesty of the other, and if they have a real understanding not only of the factual but also of the emotional problems involved, they will, over the next few years, make the transition to a relationship whose potentialities have been only dimly perceived: genuine union-management cooperation.

8

The Significance of
Scanlon's Contribution

I HAVE BEEN THINKING about three remarkable men whom I have had the privilege to know during my lifetime. One of them was a Jew who came out of the ghettos of Europe. He was born before the turn of the century, became a professor of psychology at the University of Berlin, left there along with Albert Einstein back in the early thirties when the handwriting on the wall became clear. He lived and worked in this country until his death about ten years ago. He was a remarkable innovator—a man who has had as much influence as any man in his profession on the field of psychology during the last generation. His name was Kurt Lewin, and he was the father of what we now refer to as *group dynamics*—the study of what goes on in the face-to-

First published as Chapter 2 in Frederick G. Lesieur (Ed.), *The Scanlon Plan: A Frontier in Labor-Management Cooperation.* New York: The Technology Press and John Wiley & Sons, 1958 (fifth printing by The M.I.T. Press, Cambridge, Mass., 1964).

face group and of the kinds of things that affect productivity and effectiveness and group morale.

The second man was an Ohio farm boy, also born in the last century, who at eighty today is a multimillionaire, a very famous man, also an innovator. He has had a profound influence on our society. His name is Charles Kettering, and he was research director of General Motors for many years. I know him because he was on the Board of Trustees of Antioch College where I was for a number of years, and I spent many hours sitting in my office discussing life with Ket.

The third man was an Irish lad of humble origin who was a prize fighter and a cost accountant; later he went to work in a steel mill, became a local-union president, then research director of the United Steelworkers of America, and finally a lecturer here at M.I.T. He was another innovator. I think time will show that he too has had a remarkable impact on our society. His name was Joseph Scanlon.

The differences between these three men are at first glance so great as to make you wonder why I even mention them in the same breath. But as I said, I have been struck with certain similarities among them which to me are impressive.

First of all, their point of view was always toward the future and never toward the past. Joe was fond of kidding people, sometimes quite seriously, about "facing the past and backing into the future." He had no use for the things that had been done, or for the milk that had been spilled; he wanted to look ahead and see what could come next. This was equally true of Kurt Lewin and is still true of Ket. Even at eighty, he is impatient with the way things are now being done, looking eagerly to what can happen next.

These three men, although they undertook things that were highly risky in terms of the chances of failure, never seemed to feel that risk was any more than an exciting challenge. The danger of failing never slowed them up, deterred them, or worried them. They were always emphasizing the chance of success. Kettering is fond of saying that he does not like the term "trial and error" because it carries the wrong implication. "You make trials, and you make mistakes, and you have errors, but you're aiming at success. What counts is the success that comes at the end of the road."

All three men had an experimental point of view. However, it was a rather unique one. It was not the experimental point of view of the physicist in the laboratory nearly so much as it was a practical concern with life itself. I have heard Ket say that, with respect to the inventions in the automotive field that he has been concerned with, there were no formulas, no scientific laws that could give him the answers he was seeking. He had to turn to the engine. He said: "When you want to find out how to design a high-compression head, you can't find out with a slide rule how to cut the spaces in the head; you have to ask the engine—make a head, fit it on, and see how it runs."

Kurt Lewin was fond of what he called "action research." Though he fostered much research in the laboratory, he liked to get out into the field and deal experimentally with real-life situations. And Joe Scanlon operated exclusively with this kind of experimental approach to the real life of industry.

None of these three men was ever intimidated by "what is known." There are many things in books that are not so. Those who are wise enough to realize this do not depend too heavily on the books for their answers. Again I think of many stories I have heard Ket tell about his experiences, for example, with the diesel engine. He was told by physical scientists at eminent institutions that the ideas he was working with were impossible—that he could not design an engine to do the things he was asking an engine to do. Ket tells with some amusement about talking to famous physicists about the principles that he finally used in the design of the diesel engine, and hearing them say they would not work, at a time when Ket was able to reply: "There goes one down the track."

Kurt Lewin was the same way in his work with groups. If he had depended exclusively on what was in the books, he probably would have been deterred even before he started in the important work he carried on. In the books he could find a lot about how a group was simply a collection of individuals, that all he needed to do was study them individually and then put them together, and that the sum of their individual efforts would give him his answers. Kurt knew from his observations of life that a group was more than a sum of individuals; his experiments helped to prove this and to show why. He contributed to human knowledge because he was able to put the books in perspective, read them, but not be intimidated by them.

In the same way, Joe, with his approach (for example, to the problems of incentives), was not a bit intimidated by the fact that we have thousands of volumes on incentives and on industrial-engineering practices related to them. He was prepared to go beyond these because his knowledge of life was such that he knew the books did not have all the answers.

I remember one experience with Kettering along this line which illustrates how he felt about this whole matter. I went to him for financial help for Antioch, and after some discussion he agreed to give us a library. The very fact that Ket would give a library was in itself an interesting thing. When

I was talking with him later, when the library was being designed, I said: "Ket, what do you want inscribed over the door?" He looked at me for a moment, and then he grinned as he said: "You won't do it, but I'll tell you what I'd like over the door—Enter Here at Your Own Risk."

Kettering's research over the years included much that was going on at the Antioch campus under his auspices. He had people studying about why plants are green—the subject of photosynthesis—which Ket believes in the long run is going to lead us to an understanding of sources of energy that will make atomic energy look like peanuts. This research is still in its early phases, but it is being actively pursued in the Kettering Laboratory at Antioch, among other places. Ket's way of handling his staff on this project reflected this same idea. Whenever they hit on a new notion of something to do experimentally, he would say: "Let's try it first, and then go see if other people have done it." The normal process is the reverse of this. His fear was that in going too soon to see what was in the books his staff might put on blinders and never see the possibilities. This was also a characteristic of Joe Scanlon that I very much admired.

There are two other qualities about these three people that have stuck in my mind, and they are far more important than any I have mentioned so far. One was an abiding faith in their fellow men. They did not see themselves as elite and the rest of the world as a mass of ignorant people. Each of these three great men was simply a human being in his dealings with other people. (I speak of Ket in the past tense, but at eighty he is still as alive and active as a man can be. The other two having passed on, it is difficult to use the right tense in referring to all three.)

I remember an experience Kettering had when a ship was being built and one of his first diesel engines was being installed in it. As he was wandering around the shipyard just a few weeks before the launching, he noticed one of the workmen standing at the stern of this vessel looking at it. Ket walked up to him, got into a conversation with him, hauled up a nail keg, and sat down for a while. He had noticed the man staring intently at the stern of the ship and finally asked: "What are you looking at?" The fellow said: "That propeller." Ket said: "What about it?" He said: "It's too big." Ket said: "How much too big?" "Oh," he said, "at least five inches; maybe five and a half."

I think most people would have dismissed such a comment at this point. This was an ordinary workman; he was not a member of management; he was not an architect—just an ordinary guy. But Ket did not drop the subject. He called up the architects and asked them to check the plans and find out the diameter of the propeller on this ship. They did and after a little while came back with an answer. Then he said: "Will you send somebody out to measure it?" And of course they did. Somewhat later he got a phone call, very shamefacedly, from the architectural firm. They said they did not know who had made the mistake, but the diameter of that propeller was five and a quarter inches too great! Under the conditions of design of this ship, this was a serious error. This kind of belief in the intelligence of his fellow men was as characteristic of Joe Scanlon and Kurt Lewin as it is of Kettering.

Finally, all of these things I have mentioned indicate to me in these three people, as in others like them, a way of life, a personal philosophy, and a view of what people are like and how one deals with them. This "philosophy" leads to an attitude toward risk and mistake making, to an optimism about what can be done, a refusal to think that anything is impossible, no matter how difficult it looks. It seems to me that, even though the differences are sharp, the similarities among these three innovative men are worth some reflection.

Several people have raised a question with me when the Scanlon Plan has been under discussion. They have asked: "Why is it, if the Scanlon Plan is so good, that it isn't more widely adopted?" I should like to comment just a moment on this. If you as management are considering the development of a new product or process in industry, you expect without question to devote a lot of time, money, and energy to turning your initial idea into a working process or a finished product that can go on the market. The initial idea is very remote from the final product that appears on the market.

However, when we turn to look at the problems of managing people or to matters having to do with the organization of human effort, we find management attempting (quite unconsciously, I think) to shortcut this process completely and to assume that you can go from the original idea directly to the sale or use of the product without any intervening development process. For me, the growth of the Scanlon Plan since the middle thirties represents a kind of development research that is still far from complete. This research has gone on in many companies rather than in one. There have been mistakes, there has been a lot of money, time, and energy put into it, and there will have to be a lot more before we realize the full potential of this complex and intricate set of ideas involved in Joe Scanlon's philosophy.

I have heard, over the days of the conference here, a number of questions implying that you wanted to have all the uncertainty taken out. Some of you seem to be saying: "If it's a good idea, tell me the gimmick; tell me how I can do it without any fear of failure; tell me how I can remove all the possible mistakes so that, when I go home and attempt to apply it, there'll be no risk involved." Now nobody said this in so many words, but this was the implication I got from some of the things that you said to each other. I should like to urge you to consider my analogy and realize that we are still at the pilot-plant stage. These things we are talking about—this way of life, if you like—that are represented by Scanlon and his ideas are still being developed. There is still risk for the innovators. The implication of this is that you are being asked to go out on the end of a springboard to jump off in pitch darkness, not knowing whether there is water or rocks underneath you. I do not think this is the case either.

Over the years, the thing that has fascinated me most about Joe Scanlon and the pilot plants that some of you have been operating is the similarity between the insights that you are developing and some of the ideas that have been coming out of research in the social sciences focused on people. The way these insights have coincided with our increasing scientific knowledge in this field has been to me an exciting and fascinating thing to follow. I should like to mention before I close just a few that have struck me particularly, because of the parallel between the Scanlon Plan and what is going on—entirely independent of Scanlon's operations—within the social-science field and within the broad field of management.

First, consider with me the knowledge and the insights that we have acquired within the last fifteen or twenty years about delegation and decentralization within industrial organizations. We have learned that, if we push decision making down in an organization as far as we possibly can, we tend to get better decisions, people tend to grow and to develop more rapidly, and they are motivated more effectively. Most companies today of any size at all are persuaded that the principles of decentralization and delegation—applied with wisdom—are fundamental to the successful operation of their organizations. We recognize that no small group of management or no single manager can have all the answers; even if he does have them, he will lose a great deal if he attempts to make all the decisions. He will never have an organization that grows and becomes healthy in its own right.

For me this idea, although unrelated to the Scanlon Plan, is remarkably similar in some of its implications. What Joe Scanlon was driving for was broad decentralization and genuine delegation, clear to the bottom of the organization. Some of you have given evidence of what happens when this idea is applied in that way.

There have been many developments in the social sciences in the last fifteen to twenty years having to do with motivation. We are coming around to very different notions about why people behave the way they do and about what motivates them. I am not going into this matter here, but I should like to mention that there has been much more evidence than we ever had before concerning the importance of the *social* motives of human beings. Man is still tremendously motivated to work with his fellows, to gain their recognition, their acceptance; the motivations existent in a social group are powerful in influencing behavior.

Those of you who knew Joe have heard him say many times that these social motivations, with their constructive and positive implications, have a great deal to offer management and workers alike. They are far more effective than what Joe called the "vicious" motivations stimulated by our attempt to use the carrot and stick with the typical individual-incentive approach to motivation.

We have learned a great deal in recent years about the organization of work, and we have come to realize that the typical industrial-engineering approach—the "scientific-management" approach—of the last half century, which takes all the human elements out of work and turns man essentially into a glorified machine tool, is a waste of the most important resource of the organization. You see today in the concept of job enlargement and similar ideas (again entirely divorced from the Scanlon Plan) the same concern with using the knowledge, the skill, the ingenuity, and the ability of the individual with respect to his own job, and the same concern with building responsibility back into jobs that we have defined far too narrowly.

We have had at M.I.T. for a number of years an activity that some people might regard as industrial engineering. The faculty members who head it refer to it as "the management of improvement." They have made a sharp break with traditional industrial-engineering approaches. They are concerned with participative methods that can be used to improve performance on the job. Here is something right here at M.I.T. which has been completely independent of the Scanlon Plan but which has gone parallel with it to a remarkable degree.

Finally, there is one other independent development that parallels Joe's work. It is the notion that, by and large, people are capable of being mature adults in their relationships with each other—that they are capable of *self*-direction, of *self*-discipline, of *self*-control. Our whole managerial philosophy for the past several centuries has been built on the notion that people are like children, incapable of directing their own activities within the organization, incapable of controlling and disciplining themselves. If we take this point of view, the task of management must be that of directing them, manipulating them, and controlling them in doing the job that has to be done.

I think we are beginning to get evidence from a variety of sources that this is not true, and I suspect that our conception of management as a manipulative, directive process is one day going to be supplanted by a very different notion that people are, after all, adults and capable of self-direction. When we begin to treat them that way, we shall have some different consequences in organizational behavior.

Much of the behavior we see in typical industrial organizations today is not a consequence of human nature; it is a consequence of the way we organize, of the way we manage people. Resistance to output, antagonism to management, and all kinds of subtle ways of defeating the purposes of the organization are not inherent expressions of human nature; they are results—consequences of the fact that we have built organizations and methods of control that bring about exactly these behaviors.

We have evidence in the companies that are experimenting with the Scanlon Plan concerning the different behavior you begin to get when you set up a different kind of organization with a different management philosophy, based on the idea that people are, after all, capable of behaving like adults. We have heard illustration after illustration that on the surface sound pretty odd. Says one man: "We don't have fights any more about moving a man from this operation to that one. He doesn't quarrel about the limits of his job; we don't have to go back to the contract to see whether he can be moved around." We have heard examples of people helping each other on their jobs. When one fellow runs out of work he goes over and helps another man on with his job. We have been told that the issue of management prerogatives has ceased to be an issue.

To my way of thinking, what really is being said is that, when we set up a different way of life in the industrial organization, we can expect people to behave differently. And this is exactly what some of you have discovered. It looks strange to those on the outside whose experience has been different. Perhaps it explains why some of us are worried about the legal limits we would have to put on the Scanlon agreement to make sure that this or that or the other thing does not happen. We are habituated to seeing people respond in certain ways to the typical managerial philosophy that we have been using for so long.

I should mention, before I close, one important caution to any of you who perhaps are thinking of shifting in the direction of this different way of life, this way of treating people as if they were capable adults. It is simply this: we cannot learn to run until we have learned to walk. It takes time and lots of mistakes before we can grow from the pattern that we may be accustomed to, of treating people like children and having them respond like children, to the pattern of having them react like adults.

It is easy enough, of course, to use this as an excuse to continue past practices. But even if you adopt a way of life that is built on a genuine belief that people can grow, can learn together, and can solve their mutual problems together, you must still expect the process to take some time. And the spotty picture that we have seen among the companies represented here—different degrees of success and failure, different experiences, different kinds of mistakes that have been lived through—simply reflects this natural but difficult process of growth and development that goes on when one attempts to practice a new managerial philosophy.

I should like to close by reminding you once more of my initial comment about the three men: Kurt Lewin, Charles Kettering, Joe Scanlon. In my honest opinion these were three great men. They had many qualities of greatness among them, but the most important one, the one that will make them stand out through the years, was their abiding conviction that they and their fellow men together could achieve the impossible.

9

The Scanlon Plan Through a
Psychologist's Eyes

THE SCANLON PLAN is a philosophy of organization. It is not a program in the usual sense; it is a way of life—for the management, for the union, and for every individual employee. Because it is a way of life, it affects virtually every aspect of the operation of the organization. In this fact lies its real significance.

Underlying Joseph Scanlon's efforts was a deep and fundamental belief in the worth of the human individual, in his capacity for growth and learning, in his ability to contribute significantly "with his head as well as his hands" to the success of the company that employs him. Scanlon, unlike many who make similar professions, really respected human beings.

First published as Chapter 8 in Frederick G. Lesieur (Ed.), *The Scanlon Plan: A Frontier in Labor-Management Cooperation*. New York: The Technology Press and John Wiley & Sons, 1958 (fifth printing by The M.I.T. Press, Cambridge, Mass., 1964).

The Scanlon Plan is what he evolved out of his experience to implement his fundamental belief in people. Although he was anything but a theoretician and although he was only casually familiar with the research findings of the social sciences, the plan he conceived fulfills to a remarkable degree the requirements for effective organized human effort that have been highlighted by such research. In addition, the actual experiences of Scanlon Plan companies provide significant verification of the predictions the social scientist makes on theoretical grounds.

The plan implements Scanlon's underlying belief by establishing three broad conditions within which it becomes possible and natural for all members of the firm to collaborate in contributing to its economic effectiveness. These conditions are:

1. A formally established "area of collaboration" and machinery (production and screening committees) for coordinating such collaborative efforts throughout the whole organization. This is accomplished without undermining collective bargaining or weakening the local union.
2. A meaningful, realistic, common objective (the "ratio") in terms of which such collaborative efforts can be objectively measured.
3. A psychologically adequate system of rewards (noneconomic as well as economic) for a wide range of contributions to the effectiveness of the enterprise. (Traditional incentive wages, profit sharing, and suggestion-system awards are quite inadequate in terms of modern psychological theory.)

As a consequence of establishing these three conditions, the employees and the managements of Scanlon Plan companies literally discover a new way of life. The process is not easy; some of the learning is rough indeed. There is little of a sentimental sweetness-and-light atmosphere, but there develops a mutual respect that cuts across even the most violent disagreements. The new relationship permeates in surprising but meaningful ways into every corner of the organization. It is some of these consequences and their relation to social-science theory and findings that I would like to examine.

Scientific Management and Human Capabilities

Many research studies have pointed out that, however persuasive the *logic* of "scientific management" may be, the consequences of its application are often contrary to expectation.[1] Informal but effective collusion to defeat managerial purposes takes many forms, and it is widespread. Less recognized, but perhaps more important than these consequences, is the failure of this approach to make effective use of the potentialities of people. Treating the worker as though he were, in Drucker's words, a "glorified machine tool"[2] is a shameful waste of the very characteristics that distinguish people from machines.

Despite protests to the contrary, the approach of scientific management has been to treat the worker as a "hand" rather than a human being. The consequences of so doing have been attributed to the "natural" cussedness of workers and explained as the price of technological efficiency. Pleasant working surroundings and fringe benefits have been used to alleviate the negative aspects of assembly-line jobs. Fancy

[1] Chris Argyris, *Personality and Organization*. New York: Harper and Brothers, 1957. Chaps. 4 and 5 summarize the data succinctly.
[2] Peter Drucker, *The Practice of Management*. New York: Harper and Brothers, 1954, pp. 280 ff.

communications programs and Madison Avenue sales gimmicks have been used to persuade the worker of the vital importance of his tiny contribution to the enterprise. These are understandable but largely ineffective palliatives. However, work simplification and all the other paraphernalia of the industrial engineer—consistent with a view of the worker as a glorified machine tool—remain the commonly accepted way to utilize human effort in industry.

Scanlon knew better. He knew that what Drucker calls "industrial citizenship" [3] is perfectly possible even in the mass-production setting, provided management will recognize that workers have brains and ingenuity as well as muscles. The Scanlon Plan creates the necessary conditions for this discovery. Once these conditions are established, people collaborate because it is to their interest to do so. They don't need to be made to "feel" important; they *are* important and they know it.

The most far-reaching consequence of this creation of genuine industrial citizenship is the virtual elimination of what Argyris calls the sense of "psychological failure" created by the traditional approach of scientific management. Among other things, the notion of the "nonproductive" worker, and the "burden" concept of staff and administrative employees go out the window. Productivity, under the Scanlon Plan, is not confined to direct production workers, nor is the line organization the only part of the enterprise that is seen as carrying its own weight. Productivity is measured by reduction of the labor bill, and *everyone* can contribute to this objective.

Improvement of the ratio, by every means, is everybody's business. The individual's contribution is not limited to do-

[3] Peter Drucker, *The New Society*. New York: Harper and Brothers, 1949, pp. 151 ff.

ing "a fair day's work." The janitor and the stenographer, as well as the engineer and the manager, can, and often do, exercise human ingenuity in developing improvements entirely outside the limits of their own job descriptions. The area for collaboration covers anything that will contribute to the effectiveness of the enterprise.

The challenging opportunities that are inherent in every industrial organization for people to assume responsibility, achieve status, acquire new skills, learn, develop, exercise creativity become apparent once this area of collaboration is carved out. The idea that workers are paid to do what they are told and management is paid to tell them not only prevents effective collaboration but automatically creates the feeling of psychological failure. It leads either to indifferent passivity or to active hostility. Genuine participation in problem solving removes the causes of these common reactions.

The Task of Management

It should not be supposed that management loses it responsibility to manage under a Scanlon Plan. Much to the contrary. One of the happier consequences is that the foreman ceases to occupy the impossible role that has been his in recent years and becomes a manager in the real sense of the term. He is no longer caught in the problem of divided loyalties and conflicting pressures. He is no longer the pawn of a variety of staff groups who "control" him to death under the label of serving him. He ceases to be a paper shuffler, an ineffective disciplinarian, a "master and victim of doubletalk," [4] and becomes a manager willy-nilly. Sometimes the pressures that bring about this transformation are

[4] Fritz Roethlisberger, "The Foreman: Master and Victim of Doubltalk." *Harvard Business Review*, 1945, *23*, No. 3, 283–298.

painful in the extreme. However, most supervisors come to relish their new role.

Further up the line, there is considerably less tilting with the windmill of prerogatives and more genuine concern with managing the enterprise. One of the interesting phenomena among management people in Scanlon Plan companies is their inability to comprehend the questions that are frequently asked of them concerning their freedom to manage. Authority in the sense of the right to be arbitrary, to force subordinates to do their bidding, ceases to be a meaningful idea because the collaborative relationship almost eliminates the necessity for this kind of order giving.

The management task in Scanlon Plan companies becomes one of genuine leadership. The manager who is primarily a power seeker and a protector of management's right to be arbitrary finds little satisfaction in such a situation. The pattern of managerial behavior which tends to emerge is remarkably close to that of the "democratic" leader in the classic Lewin and Lippitt research.[5] However, this term "democratic" does not mean abdication; it does not imply that "everyone decides everything." Its essence is that it makes effective use of human resources through participation; it provides general rather than close supervision; it is "employee-centered";[6] it encourages responsible behavior and tough-minded self-control rather than reliance on external authority.

As mentioned above, disagreements flourish in Scanlon Plan companies. Management has the responsibility and exercises the authority in their resolution. The difference is

[5] Kurt Lewin, Ronald Lippitt, and Ralph K. White, "Patterns of Aggressive Behavior in Experimentally Created Social Climates." *Journal of Social Psychology*, 1939, *10*, 271–299.

[6] Rensis Likert, "Motivational Dimensions of Administration." In *America's Manpower Crisis*. Chicago: Public Administration Service, 1956.

that people usually disagree about the best way to do the job or to reduce costs or to improve the profit margin rather than about whose rights are what or what legalistic interpretation should be put on a work rule. This is a big difference.

The Scanlon Plan typifies Drucker's "management by objectives and self-control." General (as opposed to close) supervision and wide delegation evolve naturally as management discovers that it is no longer necessary to force people to do what needs to be done. It becomes possible to deal with people as mature adults rather than as children and thus to avoid much of the conflict between organizational requirements and the needs of the human personality which Argyris has so well delineated.[7]

Cooperation and Competition

The psychological significance of all of this is that the Scanlon Plan "fits together" the purposes of organization with the natural human tendency to collaborate when collaboration is the sensible way to do things. Industrial organizations are complex *interdependent* human entities. Unless the many related functions are smoothly interlocked, unless people are constantly adjusting to each other in terms of common objectives, organizations cannot operate effectively.

Emphasis on individual competition, on narrow job responsibilities, and antagonism toward the natural tendency of humans to form groups characterize much of present-day managerial practice. This emphasis is 180 degrees out of phase with the need for collaboration in a complex system of interdependence.

[7] Argyris, *op. cit.*

The Scanlon Plan sets a meaningful common objective and creates the necessary conditions to bring practice and organizational need into phase. Instead of lip service to "teamwork" within a system that stacks the cards against it, the Scanlon Plan makes teamwork the natural way of life. And then it becomes no longer necessary to preach about its value!

Competitive motivations—also natural to humans—are not ignored either. However, instead of competing with fellow workers, or saying, "To hell with the other department (or the other shift); I'm paid to do my job, not to worry about them," the competition is with other companies in the industry. In a capitalist economy what could be more natural?

Resistance to Change

A fair amount of research has pointed up the fact that resistance to change is a reaction primarily to certain methods of instituting change rather than an inherent human characteristic.[8] Leo Moore and Herbert Goodwin of the M.I.T. School of Industrial Management have coined the term "improvement management" to describe a way of gaining some of the benefits of scientific management without producing resistance to change.[9] The Scanlon Plan minimizes such resistance because it involves people in the process of creating change rather than imposing it on them. Improvement management is the Scanlon way of life because everyone is interested in improving the ratio.

Significant examples of worker-generated change in the organization of work are common in Scanlon Plan com-

[8] Alvin Zander, "Resistance to Change: Its Analysis and Prevention." *Advanced Management*, 1950, *15*, No. 1, 9–11.

[9] Leo Moore, "Too Much Management, Too Little Change." *Harvard Business Review*, 1956, *34*, No. 1, 41–48.

panies. Ironically, these are frequently changes that management tried unsuccessfully to introduce in pre-Scanlon days. Resistance becomes instead active instigation. In fact, the experience of Scanlon Plan companies with the change process is one of the most clear-cut examples of the way in which the research-based predictions of social science are fulfilled in practice.[10]

It is perhaps needless to point out that restriction of output, feather bedding, collusion to "fudge" production records, and all the other ingenious group methods of defeating the managerial purposes of traditional incentive plans disappear completely in Scanlon Plan companies. Again, this is exactly what the social scientist would predict on the basis of his research into the causes of these phenomena.[11]

Human Motivation

Examination of modern theories of motivation points up even further Scanlon's insight into human behavior. The Scanlon Plan production and screening committees, as well as the whole management-employee relationship that develops, provide ideal means for satisfying ego and self-actualization needs which are typically frustrated under the conditions of present-day industrial employment.[12]

[10] See, for example, Lester Coch and John R. P. French, Jr., "Overcoming Resistance to Change." *Human Relations*, 1948, *1*, 512–532; Kurt Lewin, "Group Decision and Social Change." In G. E. Swanson (Ed.), *Readings in Social Psychology*. Rev. Ed. New York: Henry Holt, 1952, pp. 459–473; A. T. M. Wilson, "Some Contrasting Socio-Technical Production Systems." *The Manager*, 1955, *23*, 979–986.

[11] William Foote Whyte, *Money and Motivation*. New York: Harper and Brothers, 1955.

[12] Abraham Maslow, *Motivation and Personality*. New York: Harper and Brothers, 1954, especially Chaps. 4, 5, 8; Douglas McGregor, "The Human Side of Enterprise." *Management Review*, 1957, *46*, No. 11, 22–28; E. Wight Bakke, *The Unemployed Worker*. New Haven: Yale University Press, 1940; Robert W. White, *Lives in Progress*. New York: Dryden Press, 1952.

There is no undervaluation of economic motives either. However, one happy consequence of the Scanlon Plan is the minimization of conflict over the workers' share of the proceeds of enterprise. The ratio is determined from accounting data, and even in unionized companies there is no instance on record of an impasse over this issue! [13]

The economic rewards of the Scanlon Plan are fully consistent with present-day psychological knowledge. First, they are related to factors in the work situation that are controllable by employees. This is in contrast to most profit-sharing plans. Under the latter, workers are rewarded in a fashion that is only remotely connected to their direct contribution. (I know of one profit-sharing plan where the profits that were shared for several years resulted primarily from the speculation of the treasurer of the company in the raw-materials market!)

Second, the payoff is within a sensible time span. It is well established that rewards become less effective the more remote in time they are from the behavior that is being rewarded. An annual payoff (typical under profit sharing) is too remote to be of much use as a motivator. The monthly payoff under the Scanlon Plan is meaningfully related in time to the behavior that affects the ratio.

Third, the plant-wide nature of the bonus is realistic in terms of the common objectives of the members of the enterprise. It does not eliminate individual differences in wage rates related to job responsibilities, but it creates the proper perception of "sharing" in a common endeavor.

[13] Scanlon was insistent—and wisely so—that the plan offer management no escape from meeting the standards of wage levels and other conditions of employment established generally by collective bargaining. To use it in this fashion would be the surest way to undermine the union's acceptance of the philosophy of collaboration. The Scanlon Plan would quickly be seen as a device to negate the legitimate gains of the labor movement.

Fourth, the bonus is paid for *all* contributions to the effectiveness of the enterprise, rather than for the narrow contribution of output per man-hour, which is common under conventional incentive plans. There are no problems in relating pay to fancy (and largely unrealistic) "standards" for measuring individual performance, particularly for maintenance, clerical, and other service jobs. Moreover, there is no longer any incentive to defeat the time-study engineer or to hide jigs and fixtures that have been invented to "beat the standard," or to establish collusive relations with tool-crib clerks, timekeepers, inspectors, and others in order to "make out." [14]

Finally, the payoff reflects the success of the enterprise in understandable terms. There is no necessity for interpreting the elaborate formulas of the industrial engineers (which workers are quite able to do, by the way), or for fathoming the formalized and often misleading gobbledygook of the balance sheet.

Mention of the balance sheet leads to one other economic point I would emphasize: the education for all participants in the economics of enterprise. American management has spent many millions of dollars in attempts to provide economic education to workers. The results have not been measured, but one may be permitted a certain skepticism.[15]

The Scanlon Plan, however, provides such education in the most direct fashion: through day-by-day involvement in the problems of the enterprise. A casual conversation with employees of a Scanlon Plan company often reveals an understanding of our economic system that is uncommon even

14 William Foote Whyte, *op. cit.*, particularly Chap. 7.
15 William H. Whyte, *Is Anybody Listening.* New York: Simon & Schuster, 1952; Douglas Williams, in *Management Education for Itself and Its Employees.* New York: American Management Association, 1954, Part 4.

among college graduates. And this fundamental and important educative process costs not one cent! It requires no films or brochures or discussion groups or lecturers. It is obtained in the normal course of daily life by direct, first-hand experience. The employees of a Scanlon Plan company are believers in capitalism, and they know *why* they are!

Staff-Line Conflict

Friction between workers and lower levels of supervision, on the one hand, and staff departments such as industrial engineering, accounting, personnel, inspection, inventory control, purchasing, and research and development, on the other hand, is widespread in industry today, and it is a good deal more costly than management usually recognizes. Research studies and reports of participant observers have provided substantial evidence of these phenomena.[16]

A major cause of these frictions is the fact that staff departments are placed in the position of imposing their standards, their plans and procedures, their "expertness" on the line. This is a fact quite generally, despite textbook assertions that the staff functions are those of service, advice, and counsel. The staff engineer tells the worker to "follow the blueprint" even when (as happens all too often) the worker's knowledge of his tools and materials tells him that this is foolish or impossible. A substantial amount of paper work by the supervisor is summarized or scrutinized by the

[16] William Foote Whyte, *op. cit.*; Chris Argyris, "Human Problems with Budgets." *Harvard Business Review*, 1953, *31*, No. 1, 97–110; Charles A. Myers and John G. Turnbull, "Line and Staff in Industrial Relations." *Harvard Business Review*, 1956, *34*, No. 4, 113–124; and F. J. Roethlisberger and William J. Dickson, *Management and the Worker*. Cambridge, Mass.: Harvard University Press, 1939, Part IV.

accounting department and turned over to others higher in the organization to be used frequently in a disciplinary manner ("Your variances are out of line," or "You have overrun your budget," or "You made an unauthorized expenditure").

The simple psychological fact is that external controls of this kind engender hostility and lead to the exercise of a substantial degree of ingenuity directed solely toward defeating the purposes of those who have instigated the controls. This is the exact opposite of management's desire; it is the antithesis of collaboration. Unfortunately, management at the top is rarely aware of the extensiveness of this internecine warfare, and the staff groups tend to interpret it as evidence of the stupidity or inherent hostility of workers and supervisors. The typical staff reaction is to tighten and elaborate the controls, which of course simply makes matters worse.[17]

The Scanlon Plan, when these groups are included, creates entirely different relations between staff and line. The need for external controls diminishes to the vanishing point as collaboration toward the common objective of improving the ratio becomes the way of life. The staff groups can help the line in a great many ways if this is what they are set up to do. The line learns to use and to value this help as soon as the staff is relieved of a function that makes them appear to be policemen and spies. Evidence for this fundamental change in relations is to be found readily in Scanlon Plan companies. One nice example was the occasion at the Lapointe Machine Tool Company when the engineers voluntarily postponed their vacations in order to prepare specifica-

[17] See Argyris, "Human Problems with Budgets," *op. cit.*, for a penetrating analysis of this set of problems.

tions for a new order so that there would be sufficient work to avoid a layoff in the factory.[18]

If the Scanlon Plan accomplished nothing else but to bring about effective collaboration between staff and line, it would be a major contribution to organizational effectiveness. But this consequence is simply one of a large number of by-products resulting from a changed way of life. It is, in addition, a convincing demonstration of the well-established psychological fact that self-control is far more effective than externally imposed authority.

Conclusion

There are other ramifications of the operation of the Scanlon Plan that fit consistently with the implications of modern social-science findings. However, those discussed above serve to document my initial assertion concerning this consistency. They demonstrate, also, the difference between the usual personnel "program" and a genuine organizational philosophy, an industrial way of life.

No doubt other patterns of relationship will be found that yield results comparable with or superior to the Scanlon Plan. It is probable that the Plan as Scanlon conceived it would be difficult to establish in some kinds of industrial situations, even if both management and union desired it. However, I will venture the prediction that we will succeed in increasing our utilization of the human potential in organizational settings only as we succeed in creating conditions that generate a meaningful way of life.

[18] Fred Lesieur tells how the machinists in this same company, during pre-Scanlon days, would receive with glee a set of engineering specifications containing a major error and build the equipment exactly "according to specs," with full knowledge that it would ultimately have to be scrapped!

Scanlon's lasting contribution is his recognition—now effectively demonstrated in action—that one cannot successfully tackle this central task of management with gimmicks or procedures or programs. The real task of management is to create conditions that result in genuine collaboration throughout the organization. To create such conditions is to establish a way of life. This is the central conclusion to which the findings of social science are pointing today. And this is the lesson that Joseph Scanlon taught us all.

PART FOUR

■

GROWTH AND DEVELOPMENT OF INDIVIDUALS AND GROUPS

10

The Staff Function in Human Relations

IT IS COMMON PRACTICE today for organizational management to use the services of staff experts in dealing with
problems of human relations. Departments of personnel administration are created, or outside consultants are hired, not
only by industrial and business concerns, but by govern-
mental agencies, philanthropic and educational institutions,
and even to a limited extent by religious organizations and
community groups. Many managements have not been entirely successful, however, in attempting to make effective
use of these services. In some instances the staff expert has
created more problems for the organization than he has
solved. Relatively few managements have clearly determined
what function they want the staff man to perform. Hap-
hazard trial and error has frequently directed developments.
The results have not always been happy.

There are as yet no final answers to the questions thus
raised. Nevertheless, we are beginning to acquire some un-

First published in the *Journal of Social Issues*, 1948, *4*, No. 3, 5–22.

derstanding of the nature of the effective staff role. It is my objective in this discussion to present, in a tentative fashion, certain conclusions reached by a group of staff men [1] who have worked in a variety of situations and observed many others, and who have been discussing critically among themselves and with other people over a period of several years the significance of their experiences. The emphasis in this discussion will be on the staff role in industrial organizations because that is where our experience has been widest. We believe, however, that our conclusions have implications for other kinds of human organizations.

Textbook discussions of the staff role are today usually expressed in about these terms. Line management has the full and final responsibility for directing the activities of the people who comprise the organization, because line management is directly responsible to the founders or owners for achieving results through those people. Consequently, line management must retain the full authority to carry out the function for which it is held responsible. This authority cannot be successfully delegated except within the line management organization. The staff role, on the other hand, is one of counsel, service and advice. The staff expert should have no authority over any part of the line organization, nor should he take any action that will interfere with line management's performances of its role.[2]

[1] The members of the Industrial Relations Section at M.I.T., especially my colleagues, Irving Knickerbocker, Alex Bavelas, Mason Haire, Charles Myers, Paul Pigors and Douglass Brown. Some of these problems have also been discussed at length with a group of experienced industrial personnel administrators and educators who are fellow members of the American Management Association.

[2] See P. Pigors and C. A. Myers, *Personnel Administration.* New York: McGraw-Hill Book Company, 1947, especially Chap. 2, for a clear statement of this distinction between line and staff. See also "Function and Scope of Personnel Administration," *Personnel,* 1947, *24,* No. 1, 5–8.

These conceptions are accepted as sound theory by a fair proportion of managements, but practice and theory do not always coincide. The head of the engineering department in one company—a man who had under him not only engineering and drafting, but large construction and maintenance units—recently expressed considerable dissatisfaction with the department of personnel administration in his company. He stated his position somewhat as follows:

I wish we could hire someone to take these personnel problems off my hands and solve them. I know that good human relations are important. However, my subordinates and I have so much to do that we can't afford the time we are spending on grievances, personnel policies, negotiations, promotions, and individual wage adjustments. What's more, I'm sick of those interminable management meetings where we discuss petty questions like wash-up time, holiday shut-downs, disciplinary warnings, and so on. Why don't we get a competent man, give him freedom to hire whatever staff he needs, and then let him handle all these matters? An expert could do a far better job than we are doing, and leave us free to get on with our work.

The point of view expressed by this man is widely held, even by members of line management who would subscribe to the textbook statement above. They tend to separate the management function into two distinct categories. On the one hand are the planning, the making of decisions, the giving of orders, the assigning of responsibilities and the supervision necessary to get the job done. Oddly, they do not seem to regard these as matters involving human relations. These problems are "management"; they are concerned with "getting out the production." In the other category are the problems that arise (such as complaints and grievances, worker objections to supervisors' actions, the negotiation of labor agreements) and the work necessary to prevent such problems from arising (such as planning and formulating policies, training supervisors, establishing shop rules, promoting employee cooperation). These things to them are human relations, and not management. They would gladly delegate the responsibility for the second category to "experts" who presumably have the skill and knowledge to handle them.

This functional division is psychologically absurd and in practice unworkable. An industrial organization is an efficient way of producing goods because it takes advantage of the possibilities of specialization of mechanical and human effort. However, as soon as specialization occurs, there arises the necessity for integrating and directing the activities of people toward the ultimate objective of the whole organization, namely, the production and sale of goods at a profit. That integration and direction of specialized human activities is the function of line management.

It is in practice impossible to separate the function of assigning work to people from the function of settling the problems that arise in getting them to perform that work. If a worker objects to his work assignment, or to the working conditions, or the shop rules, shall we ask a personnel "expert" to hear and settle the grievance? If we do, we are giving authority to someone who is not the worker's boss to tell him what he may or may not do. How long will the foreman retain control of his men if this authority is given to someone else? The foreman is responsible for the performance of his workers; the personnel man is not. Obviously, the difficulties that will arise if we attempt this splitting of unitary functions will ultimately destroy the very integration of activities that it is line management's job to maintain.

The whole idea is about as sensible as if a symphony

orchestra conductor placed two podiums on the platform, hired a second conductor, and said: "You conduct the men in the orchestra who don't like my interpretation of the music; I'll conduct the others."

Line managers have a tendency to become unduly frustrated by the fact that human beings are somewhat less docile than materials and machines. The plea of the engineering department head that was outlined above is an unrealistic attempt to escape that frustration. It is, nevertheless, the expression of an attitude that is widespread among line managers. Moreover, many companies attempt to operate along lines similar to those proposed by that engineer. The results are seldom happy.

Frequently this idea is expressed more subtly. The manager, for example, may try to get the personnel man to make a decision for which the manager himself should take the responsibility. Perhaps he will consult the staff man on a disciplinary matter, or a new shop rule, and then ask the staff man to take the action decided upon—to impose the penalty on the erring worker, or to sign and post the rule. The staff expert who expresses unwillingness to accept such responsibilities may find himself charged with failure to fulfill the requirements of his job. The logic of textbook statements is of little help at times like this. It serves merely to arouse resistance and antagonism from the line manager. On the other hand, the staff expert who accepts such line responsibilities is likely soon to find himself in an impossible position.

There are, of course, certain things that a competent staff department can and should do for line management. These "services," however, are distinctly limited to ones that do not infringe on line authority. They must be carefully scrutinized to make sure they are not in one way or another usurping responsibilities that can only be successfully assumed by line management.

For example, staff departments may successfully handle the preliminary screening of applicants for employment who meet qualifications determined by line management; they cannot successfully assume responsibility for hiring. Staff departments may successfully help line managers to plan training programs and teach them how to teach; however, except in a very limited sense, the staff departments cannot successfully undertake to train line people in the performance of their jobs. The staff man can gather facts for and interpret policy to the line managers who hear and settle grievances; he cannot "handle" grievances without undermining line management. Staff men can aid in developing methods and procedures for wage and salary determination that will be administered by line management; they cannot successfully administer wages and salaries themselves.

A second conflict between practice and theory stems from the attitudes of staff men themselves. Some personnel administrators have (and insist that they must have) authority over the line organization. Subject to the approval of the president, or of an operating vice president, they make decisions on grievances that have been heard by lower levels of management, negotiate labor agreements, formulate, install, and police the administration of personnel policies and practices, retain final approval of wage and salary increases, promotions, transfers, disciplinary penalties, discharges, and layoffs. The degree of authority exercised by such staff men runs a wide gamut. It may often be camouflaged. For example, it is relatively common practice to give line management final authority in adopting or rejecting policies formulated by the staff, but in the same breath to give the staff responsibility for obtaining line conformity with those policies, once adopted. The term usually employed is "to coordinate" the administration of policies. "Coordination" very often in practice becomes "policing."

Even in organizations where the staff role is explicitly stated to be purely advisory, the staff man sometimes exercises considerable authority over the line organization in roundabout ways. For example, it is generally accepted that the personnel administrator can be little more than a clerk unless he is given the prestige of a position in top management. Accordingly, he may report directly to the president or to an executive vice president. From this "staff" position it is possible for him to exercise indirectly a remarkable degree of authority over the line. Suppose he is unsuccessful in getting members of middle or lower management to follow his advice. If he discusses his difficulty with the line officer to whom he reports, the result may be an order from the line officer to his subordinates that accomplishes the purpose desired by the staff man. Personnel administrators presumably possessing no authority have often been directly responsible for the demotion or even removal of intractable members of line management, or for the adoption of policies or procedures that they have previously been unsuccessful in "selling" to lower levels of management. Under such conditions, it is not unusual for the staff department to be regarded by lower and middle line management as a powerful Gestapo.

There are large differences in this respect from organization to organization. Almost regardless of position in the organization, or of defined responsibilities, some staff men exercise authority over the line organization. When this happens the net effect, from the line manager's point of view, is like that of the worker whose foreman said to him: "I want your whole-hearted cooperation; you cooperate with me, or else. . . ." The line manager feels as though the staff man had said: "I am here solely to advise and counsel with you; you take my advice, or else. . . ." From the line manager's point of view, the staff man is exercising authority whether he admits it or not.

On the other hand—again almost regardless of position or defined responsibilities—some staff men are genuinely believed by line management to exercise no authority over them whatever. They are regarded as advisors, and the line manager expects to be able to take the advice or reject it without pressure from his own line superiors.

The objective that management has in mind in establishing a personnel department or hiring a personnel consultant is, in general, much more clearly understood than are the methods by which to achieve it. The objective is to create and maintain healthy human relations in the organization. In the light of the discussion above, it is apparent that the achievement of this objective requires more than the establishment of a personnel department.

Fundamentally, the creation and maintenance of healthy human relations require certain kinds of behavior on the part of line management. The philosophy, attitudes, and skills of all members of line management, as these are reflected in their everyday behavior, are the ultimate determinants of the quality of the human relations in the organization. Stated in the terms used above, the quality of the human relations will be directly determined by the way in which line management goes about integrating and directing the behavior of the people who compose the organization.

The function of the staff expert in human relations is necessarily indirect. Nevertheless, if the staff expert's aid is to be effective, it must in many cases result in changes in line management's behavior. The common "tools" of the staff expert—the techniques of personnel administration such as systems for wage and salary administration, employee benefit programs, suggestion plans, employee publications, and the like—are only for the purpose of implementing a sound line-management philosophy and a high order of line-management skill in directing the activities of people. These techniques cannot create or maintain that philosophy or those attitudes and skills. They cannot in themselves create healthy human relations.

The staff man, then, faces a dilemma. His task is to get line management to adopt the philosophy, develop the attitudes, and acquire the skills that will create and maintain healthy human relations. However, in doing so, he must not seek or accept authority over line managers, nor in any way relieve them of their primary responsibility for directing the behavior of the people who make up the organization.

In the light of these considerations, just what is the staff role? How can "advice and counsel" bring about the necessary changes in the behavior of line management? How can the staff man stay out of the trap of accepting responsibility for line functions, without being justly accused of shirking his own responsibilities to the organization? How can he accomplish what he is supposed to accomplish, without exercising authority over line management in some fashion?

These are difficult questions. There are no simple rule-of-thumb answers. Perhaps we can obtain a somewhat better understanding of the nature of the effective staff role by turning our attention for a moment to a few basic conceptions about human behavior that have direct relevance to the problem.

1. All human behavior is directed toward the satisfaction of needs.[3] From birth to death, the individual is engaged in a constant attempt to satisfy his varied, complex, and sometimes conflicting needs. Any given behavior is a resolution of forces arising in part within him and in part in the environmental situation.

2. It follows from the first assumption that the individual will change his established ways of behaving for one of two reasons: to gain increased need satisfaction or to avoid decreased need satisfaction. Changes in his behavior for either of these reasons are inevitably a consequence of the way he perceives the situation. The expected increase or decrease in need satisfaction may be illusory (from the observer's point of view). The individual may rationalize, delude himself, ignore or misinterpret facts. Nevertheless, he behaves always in accordance with his perception of his own needs and of the possibilities for satisfying them in the environmental situation.

3. Therefore, if an individual *A* wishes to bring about a change in the behavior of another individual (or group) *B*, he can do so by effecting an "augmentation" in the possibilities of need satisfaction *as B sees them*, or alternatively by effecting a "reduction" in the possibilities of

---

[3] We believe the assumptions stated in this and the following paragraphs are virtually self-evident. They are stated somewhat dogmatically in order to avoid too much verbiage. Moreover, certain qualifications of the statements are ignored in the interests of brevity and simplicity. These qualifications are not important for our present purposes.

The point of view expressed here stems from current "dynamic" psychology, from modern psychoanalytic theory, and from our own efforts to develop a workable, integrated theory of human behavior in organizations. We have been materially influenced by such people as Kurt Lewin, H. A. Murray, Thomas French, Franz Alexander (and their many associates and students), Margaret Mead, Gardner Murphy, Edward Bibring, Walter Langer, John Dollard, Carl Rogers.

need satisfaction *as B sees them*.[4] The many variants of method for inducing a behavior change—suggestion, threat, promise, physical force, reward, punishment, propaganda, education, etc.—resolve themselves ultimately into these two.

4. *A* can utilize augmentation or reduction to induce a behavior change only if, *from B's point of view*, he possesses or controls means that *B* can use for his own need satisfaction. There are many such means, of course. Among the more common ones are money and other material possessions, knowledge, skill or specialized abilities, prestige, approval, love. A pay check, a promotion, a threat of disciplinary action, praise, criticism, an order, a request —all such things are possible ways of influencing *B's* behavior, provided *A*, who uses them, controls means that *B* regards as important for satisfying his own needs. The pay check (or money) is a direct means for *B's* need satisfaction. *A* can provide or withhold it. The threat of disciplinary action depends for its effectiveness upon *A's* control of other means that *B* desires—for example, the job and its attendant rewards.

5. In everyday usage, "authority" is equated with the reductive control of means. Thus to exercise authority is to attempt to induce a behavior change by the threat (implied or stated) to withhold, or by the actual withholding of, means for *B's* need satisfaction. Whether it is the policeman, the priest, the boss, or the parent who exercises authority, he does so by reduction, insofar as our common-sense notions of authority are concerned. The

[4] This symbolic notation is adopted to prevent later confusion. *A* always refers to the individual (or group) who is attempting to induce a behavior change, and *B* always refers to the individual (or group) whose behavior is affected.

inference that B draws is that he must obey, or else suffer a reduction in need satisfaction.

It makes little difference how we define authority so long as we understand our use of the term. I shall use the phrase "reductive authority," first to remind the reader of the common usage, and second to distinguish this method of influencing behavior from methods involving augmentation. In most situations, A can utilize his control of means either augmentively or reductively. Actually he usually does both, but the emphasis is such that B perceives the one and ignores the other.

6. One final point requires elaboration before we return to our examination of the staff role. There is plenty of evidence (both experimental and common-sense) that emphasis upon reduction frequently does not induce the behavior desired by A. If one is riding a horse, it is wise to use the whip only if one holds the reins. Otherwise the horse may run, but not necessarily in the desired direction. When A utilizes reduction, he must remember that all behavior is directed toward need satisfaction. Unless A controls every alternative form of behavior available to B, the resulting behavior may satisfy B but not $A!$ A threat often serves to eliminate a particular kind of undesirable behavior, but another equally undesirable behavior (from A's point of view) may be substituted for it. Moreover, reduction tends to be frustrating, and frustration typically creates aggression. B gets angry at A, which does not help the relationship, or increase B's docility.

Many industrial managements have emphasized reductive methods, deliberately or unwittingly, in attempting to modify workers' behavior, only to discover (1) that the desired behavior does not occur but undesired alternative behaviors do, and (2) that unexpected aggressive reactions occur. A good example is the emphasis on a purely reductive approach to discipline, or to the problem of obtaining conformity to standards of performance. Many so-called "protective clauses" in labor agreements are illustrative of the consequences.

There is today a growing recognition that success in inducing behavior change requires marked emphasis on augmentation. This is particularly true if A wants to continue the relationship with B. While it is impossible to eliminate the potentiality of reduction from any relationship in which B is at all dependent, it is almost always possible to throw the emphasis upon augmentation.

Reduction is an easy and natural method that is particularly likely to be overemphasized when A possesses much power in the relationship (i.e., when A controls important means that B requires for need satisfaction. The boss, for example, usually can replace a given worker with less reduction in his own need satisfaction than the worker will suffer if he "replaces" his boss). Excessive reliance upon reduction, however, is likely to be disappointing to A. The desired behavior too often does not occur, or the consequences in terms of aggression are unfortunate, and A discovers he has defeated his own purposes.

On the other hand, it must be admitted that the successful use of augmentation is neither simple nor easy. It requires considerable ingenuity. For example, the direct provision of means for B (high wages and other material benefits) such as is typical of paternalistic managements, is far less effective than the provision of opportunities by means of which B can, *through his own efforts*, achieve greater need satisfaction.

We may return now to our original problem.

The objective of the staff expert is to help line management to create and maintain healthy human relations in the organization. He seeks to increase his own need satisfaction by achieving this objective. In order to achieve it, he usually faces the problem of getting line managers at various levels of the organization to change their behavior. For our purposes, this "behavior" includes such things as the following: their philosophy, attitudes, decisions, methods of analyzing problems, use or acceptance of personnel techniques, ways of dealing with superiors, associates, or subordinates.

It is now perhaps clear that the use of authority in the usual, reductive sense by the staff expert is an ineffective way of inducing behavior changes directed toward healthier human relations. This is perhaps the major reason for denying the staff expert "authority" over the line organization. He must limit himself to the use of augmentation just as completely as possible because only thus can he hope to achieve the objective for which he is hired. Any staff man who has used reductive methods has had the experience of watching the line manager comply with the letter of the law while violating its spirit. The line administration of personnel policies is a complex task in which the "how" is far more important than the "what." The correct "how," depending as it does upon a sound philosophy and upon the attitudes-behind-the-act, is rarely, if ever, induced by threats or punishment.

The use of augmentation by the staff expert is difficult in the extreme. The attitudes and habits of line management are the complex result of long experience with and adjustment to people. They are deep-rooted, heavily charged with emotion, frequently influenced by unconscious factors of considerable significance. If, under such circumstances, they must be changed, a high degree of professional skill is required of the staff man.

To begin with, B must have or acquire sufficient motivation to want to change his behavior.[5] Fortunately for A, line managers almost invariably are faced with problems in human relations that they have not solved to their own complete satisfaction. This gives A his opening. If he can get B to perceive him as a possible source of help in finding more effective solutions for B's human relations problems, A will be in a position to use augmentation to modify B's behavior.

Obviously the staff man who has demanded or accepted reductive authority over the line organization will not be perceived as a potential source of help. Quite the contrary! Nor will A be perceived as a source of help if he approaches B in terms of what he thinks B *should* be worrying about. He must be prepared to help B solve B's problems as B perceives them.

This is a particularly difficult point to get across to the personnel man who is excited over the potential value to the organization of his own pet project—say, a training program, a suggestion plan, or a job-evaluation progam. That this important and valuable tool that he is prepared to offer to management, and which management obviously needs, should be put aside while he helps a superintendent or a vice president with some trivial problem arouses in him only impatience. If his manner reflects his impatience, he will very probably forfeit a real opportunity to begin to build an effective staff relation with the manager in question.

In the second place, A can rarely provide help to B simply

[5] It will be helpful to utilize our symbolic device in the discussion that follows. A refers always to the staff man who is attempting to induce certain desired behavior (attitudes, skills, etc.) on the part of B, the line individual or group.

by analyzing the problem for B and offering a solution. Sometimes, of course, this is desirable. However, if the problem really involves human relations, it is more than likely that B's perception of it reflects his own lifelong history of dealing with people. His culturally determined political and economic attitudes, his emotional convictions and prejudices, his fundamental habits of adjustment in his line role (many of which have been unconsciously acquired) will all affect his perception of the problem. In fact, they may be the very factors that have until now prevented a successful solution of his problem.

Under such circumstances, an analysis and solution offered by A, however correct it may be objectively, may meet with immediate resistance. B feels he is being asked to abandon the only approach that in his eyes can yield need satisfaction: i.e., the one resulting from his perception of the situation. From B's point of view, A's analysis will threaten reduction, not offer augmentation of need satisfaction.

Objective facts and logical conclusions drawn from them are important tools of the staff man *in their proper place*. The determining facts in most human relations problems, however, are the subjective facts of B's perceptual field and of B's needs as they relate to the problem. A's objective facts, introduced improperly or at the wrong time, will have a reductive rather than an augmentive impact on B. Knowledge and skill in analysis are important means controlled by A. He must be exceedingly careful how he uses them.

The personnel department in a large manufacturing company developed an on-the-job training course for workers that appeared to be highly efficient. A pilot experiment with the method was conducted. It yielded facts that showed quite conclusively that savings of $20,000 per year could be effected by adopting this training program for all new workers in certain departments. The facts were presented to management along with a recommendation that the program be adopted. It was turned down with some rather lame excuses, and the training department, for no apparent reason, found itself "in management's doghouse." The staff group did not discover why their facts had proved to be reductive to management. They lost an opportunity to provide real staff aid by failing to explore *B's* perceptual field before introducing their own factual analysis.

Experiences like this are more common than might be supposed. Usually the staff department's factual analysis is less "convincing" than in the case just mentioned, and therefore line management is in a position to rationalize a negative answer with little difficulty. Sometimes the staff expert, particularly if he is an outside consultant, never knows why his recommendations were not accepted. From his point of view they were obviously worth while. He is likely to rationalize his failure by concluding that management was just stupid.

Fundamentally the staff man—if he is to use augmentive methods to influence line management behavior—must create a situation in which members of management can learn, rather than one in which they are taught. *B* must acquire his own insights, discover for himself (with *A's* sympathetic aid) why his behavior has been inadequate to the problem at hand, discover his own best answer, and ultimately accept full responsibility himself for making his solution work.

In this connection, *A* faces yet another trap. Awareness of the problem of *B's* perceptual field has led some staff experts to resort to a method of dubious value. If *A* has his own solution for a problem faced by *B*, he attempts to lead *B* to "discover" that solution as *B's* own. To be sure, masterminding of this kind works in many instances. However, it is potentially a dangerous boomerang. If *B* ever discovers or even suspects what is going on, the relationship may be seriously impaired. When *B* perceives *A's* actions as masterminding, *A* is promptly seen as a source of potential reduction. Protective behavior ("keep your neck in") and aggression will surely follow. Moreover, *A* is no longer trusted. *B* feels he has been tricked by dishonest tactics.

All in all, if the staff man is in a position where it is necessary that his solution be adopted by *B*, it is far safer to present his analysis openly and face *B's* resistance, than to attempt the technique of masterminding. Unless the staff man has allowed himself to be put in an untenable role by the way his responsibilities have been defined, he will rarely find himself in a situation where *B* must be forced to accept his (*A's*) solution.

In certain respects, the methods of the staff expert resemble those of the psychological therapist.[6] This is not surprising, since the objectives of both are similar. The therapist attempts to aid individuals or groups to achieve healthy personal relations, and the staff expert attempts to aid individuals or groups to achieve healthy intraorganizational relations. Both are concerned not with imposing particular attitudes or particular kinds of behavior upon *B*, but with helping *B* to eliminate difficulties, so that he can achieve health through his own efforts and in his own way.

In spite of these similarities in objectives, the role of the staff expert in an organizational setting should not be identified too closely with the role of the psychotherapist. The former confines his efforts to a very limited area—human relations within the organization—and even within that area, he is primarily concerned with the problems involved in in-

[6] Carl R. Rogers, "Significant Aspects of Client Centered Therapy." *American Psychologist*, 1946, *1*, 415–422; Franz Alexander, Thomas French, et al., *Psychoanalytic Therapy*. New York: Ronald Press, 1946.

tegrating and directing the activities of people. His emphasis is upon the more superficial aspects of human relations and not upon the deeper aspects of personal adjustment.

Sometimes, of course, deep-seated problems of personal adjustment may prevent B from coping successfully with his problems of organizational relations. This may present critical difficulties if B happens to be in a key position in management. In such cases, the staff expert is wise to limit himself to the task of getting B to seek competent psychiatric help outside the organization. Even if the staff man is himself a skilled clinical psychologist or psychiatrist, the situation is best handled in the way in which industrial medical departments handle cases requiring extended treatment: by reference to outside experts or agencies.

By and large, our experience indicates that the staff role in human relations is more happily identified with that of the educator than with that of the therapist. A's objective is to utilize his skill to create a situation in which B can learn, and to make his knowledge available so that B may utilize it to augment his own need satisfaction in ways consistent with the achievement of organizational objectives.

A way of thinking about the staff role, as conceived here, which some of us have found helpful, is in terms of a succession of goals toward which the staff man works in any relationship with line management. These goals may be thought of narrowly, in terms of a specific problem of a single line manager, or broadly, in terms of a long-range program involving a whole management organization. They are stated as goals rather than "principles," first because the methods of reaching them will necessarily vary with the circumstances, and second because, although they may be approached, they are seldom reached in practice. It is one thing to state these complex and difficult objectives; it is another thing—at least as far as our experience goes—to possess the skill to achieve them in practice.

1. The staff expert A will seek first to establish with line management B, individually and collectively, a relationship in which he is perceived as a source of possible help in solving problems of human relations. Whether he can establish such a relationship will depend partly upon his actions, partly upon the way he is fitted into the organizational structure, and finally upon the way in which his responsibilities are defined. Any hint of reductive authority attributed to him will make the achievement of this goal infinitely more difficult.

   In establishing this relationship, A will be prepared to help B solve whatever problems B is concerned about. A's own notions of what B *should* be concerned about will be kept strictly in the background, at least until the relationship has progressed to the point where A can bring them up without becoming a potential threat to B. Outside consultants sometimes make a mistake in this respect when they utilize the device of the "survey" as a way of initiating the staff relationship.

2. When B desires his help, A will attempt to explore thoroughly with B the latter's "perceptual field." What is the problem *as B sees it?* What needs of B are involved? What does B see to be the difficulties, the obstacles, the possibilities in the situation? What are B's fears, hopes, uncertainties with respect to a solution?

   At the same time, A will attempt to make clear to B his own perceptual field. What are A's objectives in his staff job? In what ways does A propose to be of help to B? What are A's relevant needs?

   A will avoid making his own analysis of the problem,

and developing his own solution. He will not attempt to "mastermind" B, but genuinely to offer his knowledge and skill to B in a mutual exploration of the problem. Even if A thinks he knows an answer, he will reserve judgment because of a sincere belief that B's own intimate knowledge of the situation is the most likely basis on which the best answer can be developed. Genuine humility in the face of the inevitable complexity of problems of human relations is one of A's most valuable attributes. Too few staff experts recognize this important fact.

3. Together A and B will examine possible alternative approaches to the solution of the problem, seeking the solution that provides the best *common* means for *mutual* need satisfaction (i.e., that action by B that simultaneously offers the greatest potential need satisfaction for B and best achieves A's objective of creating and maintaining healthy human relations).

During this process A may be able to introduce his own ideas, gather needed factual data, provide useful "tools" (e.g., relevant personnel techniques). He must be careful, however, to do so in a manner that B will perceive as augmentive. Any attempt on A's part to impose his ideas as the necessary answer, or to force B to accept his facts as correct, will certainly defeat A's purpose.

Compromises with theoretical perfection are inevitable in approaching this goal. A solution that is objectively best may in fact be poor if in B's eyes it offers too little need satisfaction. Industrial engineers, for example, often defeat their own purposes by insisting on the most "efficient" solution, regardless of B's motivation.[7]

As a matter of fact, our experience has taught us that

[7] Peter F. Drucker, "The Way to Industrial Peace." *Harper's Magazine*, November and December 1946, January 1947.

B will surprisingly often develop a better solution than A could have produced. A's most valuable function is to create a "permissive atmosphere" in which B can explore freely all possible alternatives, and exercise his own ingenuity without fear of exposing his weakness. A seeks to help B to think out loud, guiding him where necessary with his own knowledge of the field.

In group situations especially, we have found that role playing can be a powerful diagnostic tool at this stage.[8] With it, B is able to see far more clearly than otherwise the advantages and disadvantages of alternative approaches to a solution, *including his own previous ones*.

4. Having explored together with B the alternative approaches to a solution and settled upon the "best" one, A will strive to give B whatever support he needs, while B determines for himself in practice whether the agreed-upon solution is adequate. Often the solution calls for a pattern of behavior different from B's accustomed ones. In such cases B may have some anxiety. He may lack self-confidence, fear the possibility of loss of face. He may not possess the necessary degree of some essential skill. A can aid him in planning his actions by coaching him, evaluating the results of his efforts, and otherwise providing support before, during, and after the action.

At this stage also, role playing may be an effective tool, but in a different way.[9] It affords the opportunity for pre-testing a proposed solution in a safe situation, "before the chips are down." It is a means by which B can acquire some degree of skill without exposing himself unduly.

---

[8] Alex Bavelas, "Role Playing and Management Training." *Sociatry*, 1947, 2, 183–191; Leland Bradford and Ronald Lippitt, "Role Playing in Supervisory Training." *Personnel*, 1946, 22, No. 6, 3–14.

[9] Bavelas, *op. cit.*

It may help *B* to acquire the necessary self-confidence to enable him to do something that he would otherwise be unwilling to attempt.

5. Finally, *A* will seek to help *B* gradually to assume full responsibility himself for the success of the agreed-upon plan. *A's* goal at this stage is *B's* independence, *B's* confident skill in handling this and other related problems himself.

It is dangerous for *A*, in providing help, to foster *B's* dependence. To the extent that *B* becomes or remains unduly dependent on *A*, *A's* power in the relationship is increased disproportionately. *B* soon arrives at a point where he makes quite unrealistic demands upon *A* for help. Then, no matter how unreasonable *B's* demands, any failure by *A* to provide the expected help will be seen by *B* as reduction.

Dependence, in some degree, of *B* upon *A* is inevitable if *A's* attempts to help are at all successful. The problem is to prevent that dependence from becoming too great or from lasting too long. *A's* goal is not to make himself indispensable, but to improve *B's* managerial competence toward the end of healthier human relationships in the organization.

In the light of this discussion, it is perhaps clear that the staff expert's own emotional adjustment will be a critical factor in the successful performance of his role. If his own need for power is too strong, he will not be able to create or maintain an effective relationship with *B*. If he is overanxious for recognition, he is likely to prevent *B* from achieving independence, or to destroy the results of his work with *B* by seeking credit for *B's* accomplishments. The sentimental "do-gooder," who is a familiar applicant for personnel jobs, is obviously miscast for the role outlined here. So is the "expert" who is overconfident of his own knowledge and skill.

The fundamental purpose underlying all these subgoals is to create, by the method of augmentation, opportunities for *B* to change his behavior (his attitudes, his philosophy, his skills) in a direction consistent with the creation and maintenance of healthy human relations throughout the whole organization. Unless *A* himself has some ideas about what *are* healthy human relations—what philosophy of line management is essential to their development, what attitudes are desirable, what skills are necessary—he can hardly hope to accomplish this objective. Effective performance in the staff role requires some systematic theory of human relations in organizations. Without it, *A's* guidance of *B* will be blind indeed.

At the same time, *A* cannot impose his theories on *B*. If *A's* ideas are sound, *B* will adopt them because experience demonstrates that they provide better means for his own need satisfaction. If they are incorrect, or incomplete (as they must be at this stage of the development of the field of human relations), *B* can improve on them, and *A* can utilize his own experiences in the staff role as a basis for learning. This is perhaps the greatest challenge in the methods outlined above: they offer to *A* and *B* alike a valuable opportunity to learn.

When the answers are known, when human relations has become a science rather than an art, methods such as those here suggested will perhaps no longer be necessary or desirable. Today, however, the staff expert may forfeit his own opportunities to acquire greater competence if he assumes that only *B* can learn from the relationship.

In summary, the objective of the staff expert is healthy

human relations in the organization. The staff man cannot achieve this objective himself; it can only be achieved by line management, whose function it is to integrate and direct the activities of all the people who make up the organization. The quality of human relations is directly determined by the way in which line management performs its function—by the philosophy and attitudes of line management, and the reflection of that philosophy and those attitudes in policies and procedures, and above all in line managers' day-to-day behavior. Every phase of line management's job is accomplished through people; consequently, every act of management influences the quality of human relations in the organization.

Effective performance of the staff role involves getting line management to adopt a philosophy, attitudes, and ways of behaving that will create and maintain healthy human relations. For reasons we have discussed, the staff expert must, if he is to be successful, confine himself to the method of augmentation and avoid reductive authority entirely. He possesses means (skills and knowledge) that the members of line management may use for the greater satisfaction of their needs and the simultaneous improvement of human relations. In order to make it possible for line managers individually or collectively to use these means augmentively, the staff expert strives in succession:

(1) To be perceived as a source of help.
(2) To work within the frame of reference of the line manager's perceptual field.
(3) To make it possible for the line manager to select, after joint exploration of alternatives, that course of action that offers him the greatest need satisfaction consistent with the objective of healthy human relations.

(4) To provide support in necessary ways while the line manager tests the selected method and acquires the necessary skill and confidence to use it.

(5) To guide the line manager toward the point where, having acquired competence and self-confidence, he will assume voluntarily the full responsibility himself for performing his line function in a way that will maintain healthy human relations.

The implication of these considerations for other relationships—for example, that of the line manager to his own subordinates, or that of the teacher to the student—are of more than minor significance. They cannot, however, be explored in the present context without taking us too far afield. A brief comment on one point, however, is perhaps pertinent.

If the fundamental assumptions outlined earlier in this discussion are sound, it can be argued with some force that effective line management requires the utilization of methods very similar to those that have been suggested as necessary for the effective performance of the staff role. Both the staff man and the line man are attempting to influence human behavior and human attitudes. The line manager, be he foreman or president, who carries the implications inherent in these conceptions of the nature of authority over to his own job, may gain new insight into his problems of integrating and directing the activities of people.[10]

The idea that successful performance of the line function requires heavy emphasis on reductive authority, whereas

[10] The beginnings of such a trend in management philosophy are today apparent among the more progressive companies. Cf., for example, the "coordination committee" of the Standard Oil Company of New Jersey, and the practice of "consultative supervision" emphasized by General Foods Corporation.

successful performance of the staff function precludes it, demands careful and critical analysis. On the basis of our explorations of this problem, we suggest that the only significant distinction between effective performance of the two functions is in terms of the means that A controls and that B desires for satisfying his needs, and not in terms of the way in which A exercises control.

The competent staff man controls knowledge and skills; the competent line man also controls knowledge and skills and, in addition, material means (wages and other "benefits," opportunities for promotion, etc.). The successful performance of either the line or the staff function appears to require the creation of a relationship within which B can simultaneously increase his own need satisfaction and contribute more effectively to the achievement of organizational objectives. Emphasis upon augmentation rather than reduction is one important condition for the establishment of such a relationship. The genuine motivation of subordinates to cooperate with their superiors toward the achievement of organizational objectives will not occur so long as the line function is tacitly assumed to rest solely upon the line manager's exercise of reductive authority.

Thus the staff expert is challenged, not merely to acquire skill himself in the performance of the staff role, but to use his skill in such a manner that line managers will seek voluntarily to adapt his methods to their own line function.

Management Development:
The Hope and the Reality

THIS AFTERNOON I should like to discuss management development rather than training specifically. A great deal of time, energy, and money has been put into management development activities in American industry, particularly in the past decade or so. However, I would make the observation that I do not believe we are, as yet, outstandingly successful in achieving what we set out to achieve in this field. We still have a remarkable, sometimes appalling, scarcity of really competent people available to fill the key jobs that open up. We still have problems in relating various parts of our managerial organization so that they work effectively as a team. And, certainly, we are still looking for an answer to our problems, to judge from the alacrity with which we seize upon every new idea that presents itself.

Presented to a session on training during the 24th Midyear Meeting of the American Petroleum Institute's Division of Refining, in the Statler Hilton Hotel, New York, N.Y., May 28, 1959, and published in the *Proceedings* of the Institute, Section 3, *Addresses and Reports*, 1959, pp. 272–277.

Although there is a great deal of literature on the subject, I do not believe there is a very close relation between this literature and the realities of manager development. By and large, it seems to me, our statements of policy are statements of staff ideals of what *ought* to happen. When we move out into our plants and see what actually goes on there, we often find that practice and the ideal are not entirely consistent with each other.

I should like to ask you to join me in taking a critical look at our actions in the field of manager development and to consider some of the implications that I, at least, draw from these actions. This subject has been a matter of some interest to me for several years, and in this connection I have been conducting studies in various organizations. What I have to say obviously will not apply to every company or to everybody in every company. You will have to be the judge of whether or not it is meaningful in terms of your organization.

The Negative Side

I have three major impressions about management development as it is currently practiced. These impressions are outlined in the following sections.

The Manufacturing Philosophy

For years management labored under the impression that "the cream would rise to the top" and that we need not do anything about the problem of producing future competent managers. Some time after World War I, in the thirties, a number of companies began to realize that this approach was inadequate, and that they must do something about the problem. In so doing, it was almost as though they said,

"We need a product; let us set up a manufacturing organization to produce it."

If you consider the activities with which we are all familiar in the management development field in line with this analogy, I think perhaps you will agree with me that there is quite a startling similarity. Most such programs, for example, include a very elaborate market analysis. They include raw-material specifications. Through recruitment practices, the attempt is made to purchase the raw materials required for "manufacturing" managers. In addition, the following day-to-day processes in which we engage have something of this manufacturing flavor:

> Initial indoctrination
> Appraisal or inspection
> Rotation
> Training
> Promotion

I do not believe that we have been conscious and deliberate about adopting this manufacturing philosophy. On the other hand, I believe it was quite natural that management in industry, faced with the kind of problems that are present in this field, should tend to think of them in this way. The question appears to be: how do we manufacture the product we need to get the job done?

The ideal, however, which we reiterate to ourselves with some frequency, is this. Men develop themselves; the process of manager development can only be a process of self-development. It seems to me, our actions contradict the very words that we say along these lines. We take people and try to develop them, to change them, to rework them, to modify them into some kind of product that we believe our company needs. A man becomes essentially a passive agent in the process rather than an active one. To a very limited extent we may take account of the man's needs, but we do so only in the sense that *we* decide what his needs are, and we do the things that *we* believe are good for him. I think this is true, broadly, of our processes of selection, evaluation, training, and rotation; of our whole concept of promotability; and of the administration of our promotion procedures.

You say, "Of course, this is necessary—we are not in business for our health." I agree. But is it consistent with our stated ideals to do these things to people in the light of company needs exclusively, or almost exclusively? Do we know, in fact, that this is the best way to develop people? Do we know what product we are trying to develop? Could any man today tell us what the manager of 1980 is going to face? what knowledge, skills, and abilities he will require? what situations are going to be the crucial ones for him? Could any man in 1930 have made similar predictions about the manager of 1959?

My first impression, then, is that the philosophy we practice—not the one we preach—is a manufacturing philosophy in which we set up mechanical means to produce a product that we cannot define very well but nevertheless believe we need.

Neglect of the Facts of Learning

My second impression is that our management development practices in the field ignore, to a very considerable extent, several facts concerning human learning. For example, we ignore perhaps the most fundamental aspect of such learning, which is that people tend to adopt and repeat forms of behavior or actions that are rewarded, and to discard or avoid those that are punished.

Take the whole question of classroom training, for example. Even if it were true that by putting people in a classroom we could teach them to be managers, it seems to me that we ignore this problem of reward almost immediately on sending them back from the classroom. The two studies that have been at all definitive in attempting to evaluate the consequences of classroom training in this managerial area resulted in almost identical findings: (1) the effect of such training vanished almost completely within approximately 18 months; and (2) how the man was treated by his boss when he returned to his job was the critical factor in whether or not this happened.

I believe that we often shrug our shoulders over the fact that we have young men under development as managers, at various levels and in various functions of our organizations, working under superiors who are relatively incompetent. A boss who is a poor boss may have a number of bright, able, competent people who could develop a great deal under the proper leadership. Yet when this question comes up, we say, "Well, there is nothing much we can do about it."

We attach a great deal of importance to another activity in the management development field that is involved with learning, namely, rotation—moving people from job to job to broaden their experience and make them more able as managers. There are tremendous variations in company practice and a considerable number of completely unanswered questions on this subject. For example, should job rotation be limited to a single broad function within the organization and the man be given opportunity to operate in various jobs within that function? Or should we conceive of it as something in which he needs experience in a variety of functions, and move him widely throughout the organization?

At what age should we provide people with this rotational experience? When they are young and fresh and flexible and just out of school, or when they are mature and well balanced and experienced—in their forties, perhaps?

Should rotation be a matter of moving quickly into a situation, learning as much as possible about it, and moving out? Or should it be a matter of going in and taking full responsibility for the job?

Is experience the best teacher? The implication behind rotation is that this is so; yet we all know, as one of my colleagues has said, that some people can have the same experience for 15 years and learn nothing. Experience by itself does not necessarily teach anything. It is experience under certain circumstances and conditions that makes the difference. Do we, in our rotation programs, take account of these circumstances?

What about the necessity for technical knowledge on the part of the manager? There are those who say it is absolutely indispensable that a manager know a great deal about the function and activities of the organization that he is managing; others believe that managing is independent of this kind of knowledge and that the good manager can move from one function to another, from one company to another, and do equally well regardless of his technical knowledge. In my experience, I have found that we tend to make distinctions, depending on what the function is. If it is an operating job, or if it is a research management job, many of us are inclined to say that technical knowledge is indispensable. However, we will put an operating man with no training, no technical knowledge whatever, at the head of a personnel function and expect him to manage effectively. Somehow that kind of technical knowledge is not important, but manufacturing knowledge or research knowledge is.

Finally, one place where, it seems to me, we violate even our common-sense knowledge of learning quite regularly and consistently is in the field of promotion. In many instances, we have made promotion the exclusive measure of success for the individual. If you are not promotable out of your present job, you are a failure. We talk about people's having reached their ceiling. We set up a job-evaluation program, so that a person who is not promotable out of a given job has soon reached his maximum salary. In effect, we say to people by our actions, "You are of limited value to this organization unless you are capable of becoming president." Because this matter of promotability and of ceiling applies to everybody—from a vice president down—the vice president who is not promotable to president is a failure, too!

I believe it is fair to say that we need a vast heterogeneity of human resources to run our organizations in all functions and at all levels. An outstanding man at the first, second, or third level from the bottom can have tremendous value to an organization—perhaps as much value in his own way as an executive vice president in his way.

All of these things, then, lead me to raise the question of whether or not our practice is consistent with our knowledge about how people learn and about the importance of rewards for learning. Are we teaching our young men, for example, to get as quickly as they can through a given job and on to another one, or are we teaching them to exploit the possibilities inherent in every job for learning more, for discovering how to do the job better? I would argue that, by and large, we are doing the former and not the latter.

The "Burden" Concept

My third impression concerning management development activities, in contrast to stated policies, is that this development is regarded by operating managers in our organizations as a burden, an added responsibility to the job of management. I believe they show us this every day by their resistance to our programs and by their evident lack of time for these activities in the management development field. They are too busy. Too busy doing what? Too busy managing to be able to develop managers. This is evidenced by the fact that we must always "sell" them our ideas concerning management development; by the fact that we, as staff people, try to get strong backing from the top of the organization so that, if necessary, we can somehow impose our will on these managers who will not do a good job of developing their subordinates.

Here again, however, do we reward the manager who does an outstanding job of developing his subordinates, or do we ignore this in favor of the other aspects of his managerial position? I have asked the following question in dozens of companies: "To what extent is the outstanding developer of men in your management recognized, tangibly or otherwise, for that ability?" Almost without exception, there follow a shrug of the shoulders and the reaction, "Well, we value it, but I am afraid we do not do very much to recognize it in a tangible way. If a man is a good manager in the technical sense, this we recognize; however, in terms of reward, we do not necessarily consider how good he is at developing people."

The very few people who do subscribe to a policy of reward are managers who themselves are good in this field. They realize that as their subordinates become more efficient, their own jobs become easier. They are not too concerned with those rewards that may come from outside; their rewards come from seeing their own young men develop and from turning their departments into more effective units. However, in my experience, these men constitute a pitifully small minority.

All of this is by way of saying that it seems obvious to me that management development should be a natural by-product of good management, not an additional burden.

Summary

Thus, if I can summarize what I have said so far, I believe, first, that we give a good deal of lip service in our literature and stated policies to the idea that men should develop themselves, but many of our actions belie our statements, in that we use a manufacturing approach in management development—unconsciously but pervasively—although we do not really know what product we are trying to manufacture.

Second, I believe we give lip service to the idea that management development is learning of a very complex kind, but I question whether many of our actions fully teach what we expect them to teach. I do not believe we have examined as closely as we might the questions of what learning is, and under what conditions it takes place.

And, finally, although we want our managers to recognize that management development is an important responsibility, a natural part of the managerial job, we actually behave in such a fashion that they see it as a burden, a nuisance, an added responsibility which they avoid as often as they can.

Although I may have been unduly harsh in what I have said so far, I am sure that it is substantially true. I am equally sure, however, that there are variations from company to company, and from division to division, and I have certainly ignored some of the positive accomplishments in this field over the past couple of decades. For example, as a result of a real concern on the part of most top managements with the problems of developing effective successors, we have collected within our organizations a fair amount of data that tell us a good deal about what our needs are and what we must do in order to fill these needs. We have a fairly genuine commitment throughout industry today to education and its values. We have made many attempts, and are still attemping, to combat the undue specialization that leaves us with managers without the scope to do the job that must be done. And we certainly have recognized, as our predecessors perhaps did not, that good managers are not born but that, given fundamental and basic ability, many people can learn to be effective managers.

Nevertheless, in spite of these things, I remain convinced that some of our unconscious, or partly recognized, assumptions hamper us in achieving what we might be achieving in this field. In fact, I would go so far as to say that managers develop largely *in spite of*, rather than because of, the management development activities in most companies.

The Positive Side

I do not wish to be merely a destructive critic—I do have some ideas that might bring our practice a little more closely into line with our ideals. However, in the limited time at our disposal, I shall confine myself to one particular suggestion. In doing so, I must repeat that we do not know what problems the general manager of 1980, for example, will meet. Thus we can only hope to develop a variety of managerial resources, a heterogeneity of talents, to meet the kind of needs that will inevitably face us in the years ahead.

This being the case, I would advocate not the manufacturing philosophy that has been described but what might be called an "agricultural" philosophy, bearing in mind certain facts: In the first place, human beings are capable of developing in ways in which plants are not; that is, they can exert self-control as they grow. In the second place, in the management development field we can control not only the soil conditions but the climate. It is not a matter of making people become something; it is a matter of creating an environment in which people can grow. And if we adopt this kind of philosophy rather than the manufacturing philosophy, I believe we will modify many of our present practices.

Let me give you one fairly practical illustration which I believe clearly indicates the advantages of this agricultural philosophy over the manufacturing philosophy. This illustration is based on the assumption that the adult human being is capable of learning how to direct and control his own behavior in the service of objectives to which he is committed. Peter Drucker, a number of years ago, proposed an idea that has been elaborated and worked on in a number of companies recently. He talked about management by objectives and self-control, and it is within this context that the particular method that I should like briefly to describe falls. Some of my friends have called it target setting. The method may be implemented in a number of ways, but I would suggest that the following basic steps be taken:

1. The subordinate should assume the responsibility for determining what his job is, not the superior for telling him. Through discussion they should come to a mutual understanding of what the man is accountable for. Frequently this turns out to be quite a learning process for both parties.
2. The subordinate should set specific objectives for his

operation within some immediate period of time, e.g., six months. In setting and trying to achieve these objectives, he should be concerned not only with what is good for the company, but with adopting methods and devising strategies that will result in his own growth and development.

3. The subordinate should be given an appropriate degree of autonomy to accomplish his objectives. The critical factor here will be the attitude of the superior and his ability to decide whether the man requires close or "general" supervision.

4. At the end of the stated period, the man and his superior should sit down together while the subordinate evaluates his own performance with respect to the established targets.

This is but one illustration of a type of approach to managing people that I think yields some growth, some development, in the assuming of increased responsibility by the subordinates. Certainly, this method does not meet administrative requirements for formal judgments concerning the subordinate's performance; however, it does provide a basis on which the superior may make such judgments. Management development thus becomes an integral part of the job of managing, not an added burden.

And so, to re-emphasize the idea of an agricultural philosophy in management development, I suggest that perhaps if we think of ourselves more or less as the farmer does—as trying to create conditions for growth for people who have the inherent abilities, talents, and potentialities—we may make greater progress than heretofore in this field.

I 2

An Uneasy Look at Performance Appraisal

PERFORMANCE APPRAISAL within management ranks has become standard practice in many companies during the past twenty years, and is currently being adopted by many others, often as an important feature of management development programs. The more the method is used, the more uneasy I grow over the unstated assumptions that lie behind it. Moreover, with some searching, I find that a number of people, both in education and in industry, share my misgivings. This article, therefore, has two purposes:

To examine the conventional performance appraisal plan, which requires the manager to pass judgment on the personal worth of subordinates.

To describe an alternative, which places on the subordinate the primary responsibility for establishing performance goals and appraising progress toward them.

Reprinted from *Harvard Business Review*, 1957, *35*, No. 3, 89–94.

Current Programs

Formal performance appraisal plans are designed to meet three needs, one for the organization and two for the individual: (1) They provide systematic judgments to back up salary increases, promotions, transfers, and sometimes demotions or terminations. (2) They are a means of telling a subordinate how he is doing, and suggesting needed changes in his behavior, attitudes, skills, or job knowledge; they let him know "where he stands" with the boss. (3) They also are being increasingly used as a basis for the coaching and counseling of the individual by the superior.

Problem of Resistance

Personnel administrators are aware that appraisal programs tend to run into resistance from the managers who are expected to administer them. Even managers who admit the necessity of such programs frequently balk at the process—especially the interview part. As a result, some companies do not communicate appraisal results to the individual, despite the general conviction that the subordinate has a right to know his superior's opinion so he can correct his weaknesses.

The boss's resistance is usually attributed to the following causes:

A normal dislike of criticizing a subordinate (and perhaps having to argue about it).

Lack of skill needed to handle the interviews.

Dislike of a new procedure with its accompanying changes in ways of operating.

Mistrust of the validity of the appraisal instrument.

To meet this problem, formal controls—scheduling, reminders, and so on—are often instituted. It is common experience that without them fewer than half the appraisal interviews are actually held. But even controls do not necessarily work. Thus:

In one company with a well-planned and carefully administered appraisal program, an opinion poll included two questions regarding appraisals. More than 90% of those answering the questionnaire approved the idea of appraisals. They wanted to know how they stood. Some 40% went on to say that they had never had the experience of being told—yet the files showed that for over four-fifths of them a form had been signed testifying that they had been through an appraisal interview, some of them several times!

The respondents had no reason to lie, nor was there the slightest supposition that their superiors had committed forgery. The probable explanation is that the superiors, being basically resistant to the plan, had conducted the interviews in such a perfunctory manner that many subordinates did not recognize what was going on.

Training programs designed to teach the skills of appraising and interviewing do help, but they seldom eliminate managerial resistance entirely. The difficulties connected with "negative appraisals" remain a source of genuine concern. There is always some discomfort involved in telling a subordinate he is not doing well. The individual who is "coasting" during the few years prior to retirement after serving his company competently for many years presents a special dilemma to the boss who is preparing to interview him.

Nor does a shift to a form of group appraisal solve the problem. Though the group method tends to have greater validity and, properly administered, can equalize varying standards of judgment, it does not ease the difficulty inherent in the interview. In fact, the superior's discomfort is often intensified when he must base his interview on the results of a *group* discussion of the subordinate's worth. Even if the final judgments have been his, he is not free to discuss the things said by others that may have influenced him.

The Underlying Cause

What should we think about a method—however valuable for meeting organizational needs—that produces such results in a wide range of companies with a variety of appraisal plans? The problem is one that cannot be dismissed lightly.

Perhaps this intuitive managerial reaction to conventional performance appraisal plans shows a deep but unrecognized wisdom. In my view, it does not reflect anything so simple as resistance to change, or dislike for personnel technique, or lack of skill, or mistrust for rating scales. Rather, managers seem to be expressing very real misgivings, which they find difficult to put into words. This could be the underlying cause:

The conventional approach, unless handled with consummate skill and delicacy, constitutes something dangerously close to a violation of the integrity of the personality. Managers are uncomfortable when they are put in the position of "playing God." The respect we hold for the inherent value of the individual leaves us distressed when we must take responsibility for judging the personal worth of a fellow man. Yet the conventional approach to performance appraisal forces us, not only to make such judgments and to see them acted upon, but also to communicate them to those we have judged. Small wonder we resist!

The modern emphasis upon the manager as a leader who

strives to *help* his subordinates achieve both their own and the company's objectives is hardly consistent with the judicial role demanded by most appraisal plans. If the manager must put on his judicial hat occasionally, he does it reluctantly and with understandable qualms. Under such conditions it is unlikely that the subordinate will be any happier with the results than will the boss. It will not be surprising, either, if he fails to recognize that he has been told where he stands.

Of course, managers cannot escape making judgments about subordinates. Without such evaluations, salary and promotion policies cannot be administered sensibly. But are subordinates like products on an assembly line, to be accepted or rejected as a result of an inspection process? The inspection process may be made more objective or more accurate through research on the appraisal instrument, through training of the "inspectors," or through introducing group appraisal; the subordinate may be "reworked" by coaching or counseling before the final decision to accept or reject him; but as far as the assumptions of the conventional appraisal process are concerned, we still have what is practically identical with a program for product inspection.

On this interpretation, then, resistance to conventional appraisal programs is eminently sound. It reflects an unwillingness to treat human beings like physical objects. The needs of the organization are obviously important, but when they come into conflict with our convictions about the worth and the dignity of the human personality, one or the other must give.

Indeed, by the fact of their resistance, managers are saying that the organization must yield in the face of this fundamental human value. And they are thus being more sensitive than are personnel administrators and social scientists whose business it is to be concerned with the human problems of industry!

A New Approach

If this analysis is correct, the task before us is clear. We must find a new plan—not a compromise to hide the dilemma, but a bold move to resolve the issue.

A number of writers are beginning to approach the whole subject of management from the point of view of basic social values. Peter Drucker's concept of "management by objectives" [1] offers an unusually promising framework within which we can seek a solution. Several companies, notably General Mills, Incorporated, and General Electric Company, have been exploring different methods of appraisal that rest upon assumptions consistent with Drucker's philosophy.

Responsibility on Subordinate

This approach calls on the subordinate to establish short-term performance goals *for himself*. The superior enters the process actively only *after* the subordinate has (a) done a good deal of thinking about his job, (b) made a careful assessment of his own strengths and weaknesses, and (c) formulated some specific plans to accomplish his goals. The superior's role is to help the man relate his self-appraisal, his "targets," and his plans for the ensuing period to the realities of the organization.

The first step in this process is to arrive at a clear statement of the major features of the job. Rather than a formal job description, this is a document drawn up *by the subor-*

[1] See Peter Drucker, *The Practice of Management*. New York: Harper and Brothers, 1954.

dinate after studying the company-approved statement. It defines the broad areas of his responsibility as they actually work out in practice. The boss and employee discuss the draft jointly and modify it as may be necessary until both of them agree that it is adequate.

Working from this statement of responsibilities, the subordinate then establishes his goals or "targets" for a period of, say, six months. These targets are *specific* actions which the man proposes to take, i.e., setting up regular staff meetings to improve communication, reorganizing the office, completing or undertaking a certain study. Thus, they are explicitly stated and accompanied by a detailed account of the actions he proposes to take to reach them. This document is, in turn, discussed with the superior and modified until both are satisfied with it.

At the conclusion of the six-month period, the subordinate makes *his own* appraisal of what he has accomplished relative to the targets he had set earlier. He substantiates it with factual data wherever possible. The "interview" is an examination by superior and subordinate together of the subordinate's self-appraisal, and it culminates in a resetting of targets for the next six months.

Of course, the superior has veto power at each step of this process; in an organizational hierarchy anything else would be unacceptable. However, in practice he rarely needs to exercise it. Most subordinates tend to underestimate both their potentialities and their achievements. Moreover, subordinates normally have an understandable wish to satisfy their boss and are quite willing to adjust their targets or appraisals if the superior feels they are unrealistic. Actually, a much more common problem is to resist the subordinates' tendency to want the boss to tell them what to write down.

Analysis versus Appraisal

This approach to performance appraisal differs profoundly from the conventional one, for it shifts the emphasis from *appraisal* to *analysis*. This implies a more positive approach. No longer is the subordinate being examined by the superior so that his weaknesses may be determined; rather, he is examining himself, in order to define not only his weaknesses but also his strengths and potentials. The importance of this shift of emphasis should not be underestimated. It is basic to each of the specific differences that distinguish this approach from the conventional one.

The first of these differences arises from the subordinate's new role in the process. He becomes an active agent, not a passive "object." He is no longer a pawn in a chess game called management development.

Effective development of managers does not include coercing them (no matter how benevolently) into acceptance of the goals of the enterprise, nor does it mean manipulating their behavior to suit organizational needs. Rather, it calls for creating a relationship within which a man can take responsibility for developing his own potentialities, plan for himself, and learn from putting his plans into action. In the process he can gain a genuine sense of satisfaction, for he is utilizing his own capabilities to achieve simultaneously both his objectives and those of the organization. Unless this is the nature of the relationship, "development" becomes a euphemism.

Who Knows Best?

One of the main differences in this approach is that it rests on the assumption that the individual knows—or can learn—more than anyone else about his own capabilities, needs, strengths and weaknesses, and goals. In the end, only he can determine what is best for his development. The conventional approach, on the other hand, makes the assumption that the superior can know enough about the subordinate to decide what is best for him.

No available methods can provide the superior with the knowledge he needs to make such decisions. Ratings, aptitude and personality tests, and the superior's necessarily limited knowledge of the man's performance yield at best an imperfect picture. Even the most extensive psychological counseling (assuming the superior possesses the competence for it) would not solve the problem, because the product of counseling is self-insight on the part of the *counselee*.

Psychological tests are not being condemned by this statement. On the contrary, they have genuine value in competent hands. Their use by professionals as part of the process of screening applicants for employment does not raise the same questions as their use to "diagnose" the personal worth of accepted members of a management team. Even in the latter instance, the problem we are discussing would not arise if test results and interpretations were given *to the individual himself*, to be shared with superiors at his discretion.

The proper role for the superior, then, is the one that falls naturally to him under the suggested plan: helping the subordinate relate his career planning to the needs and realities of the organization. In the discussions the boss can use his knowledge of the organization to help the subordinate establish targets and methods for achieving them that will (a) lead to increased knowledge and skill, (b) contribute to organizational objectives, and (c) test the subordinate's appraisal of himself.

This is help that the subordinate wants. He knows well

that the rewards and satisfactions he seeks from his career as a manager depend on his contribution to organizational objectives. He is also aware that the superior knows more completely than he what is required for success in this organization and *under this boss*. The superior, then, is the person who can help him test the soundness of his goals and his plans for achieving them. Quite clearly the knowledge and active participation of *both* superior and subordinate are necessary components of this approach.

If the superior accepts this role, he need not become a judge of the subordinate's personal worth. He is not telling, deciding, criticizing, or praising—not "playing God." He finds himself listening, using his own knowledge of the organization as a basis for advising, guiding, encouraging his subordinates to develop their own potentialities. Incidentally, this often leads the superior to important insights about himself and his impact on others.

Looking to the Future

Another significant difference is that the emphasis is on the future rather than the past. The purpose of the plan is to establish realistic targets and to seek the most effective ways of reaching them. Appraisal thus becomes a means to a *constructive* end. The 60-year-old "coaster" can be encouraged to set performance goals for himself and to make a fair appraisal of his progress toward them. Even the subordinate who has failed can be helped to consider what moves will be best for himself. The superior rarely finds himself facing the uncomfortable prospect of denying a subordinate's personal worth. A transfer or even a demotion can be worked out without the connotation of a "sentence by the judge."

Performance versus Personality

Finally, the accent is on *performance*, on actions relative to goals. There is less tendency for the personality of the subordinate to become an issue. The superior, instead of finding himself in the position of a psychologist or a therapist, can become a coach helping the subordinate to reach his own decisions on the specific steps that will enable him to reach his targets. Such counseling as may be required demands no deep analysis of the personal motivations or basic adjustment of the subordinate. To illustrate:

Consider a subordinate who is hostile, short tempered, uncooperative, insecure. The superior need not make any psychological diagnosis. The "target setting" approach naturally directs the subordinate's attention to ways and means of obtaining better interdepartmental collaboration, reducing complaints, winning the confidence of the men under him. Rather than face the troublesome prospect of forcing his own psychological diagnosis on the subordinate, the superior can, for example, help the individual plan ways of getting "feedback" concerning his impact on his associates and subordinates as a basis for self-appraisal and self-improvement.

There is little chance that a man who is involved in a process like this will be in the dark about where he stands, or that he will forget that he is the principal participant in his own development and responsible for it.

A New Attitude

As a consequence of these differences, we may expect the growth of a different attitude toward appraisal on the part of superior and subordinate alike.

The superior will gain real satisfaction as he learns to

help his subordinates integrate their personal goals with the needs of the organization so that both are served. Once the subordinate has worked out a plan of action satisfactory to both parties, the superior can delegate to him the responsibility for putting it into effect. He will see himself in a consistent managerial role rather than in the position of being forced to adopt the basically incompatible role of either the judge or the psychologist.

Unless there is a basic personal antagonism between the two men (in which case the relationship should be terminated), the superior can conduct these interviews so that both are actively involved in seeking the right basis for constructive action. The organization, the boss, and the subordinate all stand to gain. Under such circumstances, the opportunities for learning and for genuine development of both parties are maximal.

The particular mechanics are of secondary importance. The needs of the organization in the administration of salary and promotion policies can easily be met within the framework of the analysis process. The machinery of the program can be adjusted to the situation. No universal list of rating categories is required. The complications of subjective or prejudiced judgment, of varying standards, of attempts to quantify qualitative data, all can be minimized. In fact, *no* formal machinery is required.

Problems of Judgment

I have deliberately slighted the many problems of judgment involved in administering promotions and salaries. These are by no means minor, and this approach will not automatically solve them. However, I believe that if we are prepared to recognize the fundamental problem inherent in the conventional approach, ways can be found to temper our present administrative methods.

And if this approach is accepted, the traditional ingenuity of management will lead to the invention of a variety of methods for its implementation. The mechanics of some conventional plans can be adjusted to be consistent with this point of view. Obviously, a program utilizing ratings of the personal characteristics of subordinates would not be suitable, but one that emphasizes *behavior* might be.

Of course, managerial skill is required. No method will eliminate that. This method can fail as readily as any other in the clumsy hands of insensitive or indifferent or power-seeking managers. But even the limited experience of a few companies with this approach indicates that managerial *resistance* is substantially reduced. As a consequence, it is easier to gain the collaboration of managers in developing the necessary skills.

Cost in Time

There is one unavoidable cost: the manager must spend considerably more time in implementing a program of this kind. It is not unusual to take a couple of days to work through the initial establishment of responsibilities and goals with each individual. And a periodic appraisal may require several hours rather than the typical 20 minutes.

Reaction to this cost will undoubtedly vary. The management that considers the development of its human resources to be the primary means of achieving the economic objectives of the organization will not be disturbed. It will regard the necessary guidance and coaching as among the most important functions of every superior.

Conclusion

I have sought to show that the conventional approach to performance appraisal stands condemned as a personnel method. It places the manager in the untenable position of judging the personal worth of his subordinates, and of acting on these judgments. No manager possesses, nor could he acquire, the skill necessary to carry out this responsibility effectively. Few would even be willing to accept it if they were fully aware of the implications involved.

It is this unrecognized aspect of conventional appraisal programs that produces the widespread uneasiness and even open resistance of management to appraisals and especially to the appraisal interview.

A sounder approach, which places the major responsibility on the subordinate for establishing performance goals and appraising progress toward them, avoids the major weaknesses of the old plan and benefits the organization by stimulating the development of the subordinate. It is true that more managerial skill and the investment of a considerable amount of time are required, but the greater motivation and the more effective development of subordinates can justify these added costs.

PART FIVE

THE MANAGER
AND THE
HUMAN SCIENCES

13

The Manager, Human Nature,
and Human Sciences

ANY USEFUL scientific knowledge consists in (1) identification of the factors, characteristics, or variables that
are sufficient and necessary "causes" of a given set of phenomena, and (2) statements about the relationships among
these factors that are associated with changes in the phenomena. Thus the performance (P) of an individual at work
in an industrial organization is a function of certain characteristics of the individual (including his knowledge, skills,
motivation, attitudes) and certain aspects of the environmental situation (including the nature of his job, the rewards associated with his performance, the leadership provided him).

$$P = f(I_{a,b,c,d} \ldots E_{m,n,o,p} \ldots)$$

The relationships among these variables are many and complex. Existing behavioral science knowledge does not permit

This is a chapter from a book that Douglas McGregor was working on
at the time of his death, October 13, 1964.

precise quantitative descriptions of most of them, but a lot can be said about their form and nature.

Perhaps the most general statement of the potential contribution that behavioral science can make to management would be this: our present knowledge indicates that there are a number of important characteristics of individuals *and* of the work environment that conventional management practice does not take into account. The variables that most managers do take into account are necessary, but they are not sufficient to explain organized human effort. Since these additional variables are not recognized, the relationships among them are unknown to these managers. Existing behavioral science knowledge affords the possibility of improved control of organized human effort through the inclusion of these variables and their interrelationships in managerial practice.

It is obvious, and demonstrably true scientifically, that man's behavior is influenced by certain characteristics of his environment. When we speak of motivating people, we are referring to the possibility of creating relationships between characteristics of man and characteristics of his environment that will result in certain desired behavior. "Reward" and "punishment" are the terms in common use to describe generally the environmental characteristics that are controlled in order to influence behavior.

It is important to recognize, however, that what is involved is always a relationship between E variables and I variables. Giving or withholding a particular sum of money or a particular kind of food will affect a particular individual's behavior in certain ways, depending on his characteristics. The offer of beef to a Hindu and a Christian will affect their behavior quite differently. A glass of water may have a powerful influence on a man dying of thirst and none on a man who already has access to water. A ten-dollar monthly raise in pay will affect a clerk and a top executive differently.

The relationships are indeed complex. They involve the individual's capabilities, his goals, his needs, his expectations, his attitudes, his perceptions concerning the scarcity of the reward that is being given or withheld. They involve relationships not only of reward or punishment to the individual, but of other characteristics of the environment as well. The threat of discharge will affect the behavior of an accounting clerk and a nuclear physicist differently in U.S. industry under present economic conditions. Knowledge about cause and effect in human behavior rests on knowledge of the relevant characteristics of I and E (which ones are "necessary" and which are "sufficient" to account for the behavior), and on knowledge about the relationships that hold among these characteristics.

There is a substantial amount of unified knowledge about some of these relationships today; there is less knowledge and some dispute about others, and virtually none about still others. A detailed analysis of the current status of knowledge would have little value for the manager. I propose, therefore, to present only certain general findings that seem to me to be fairly well established and, in addition, to be particularly relevant to the concerns of industrial managers. Even so, I will ignore many qualifications and complications.

An important body of knowledge has to do with two quite different kinds of motivational relationships. The first, and by far the most recognized and utilized today, involves what are called "extrinsic" rewards and punishments—they exist as characteristics of the environment of the individual, and their relationship to behavior is relatively direct. Money is the most obvious of them, but promotion, praise, recognition, criticism, social acceptance and rejection, and "fringe benefits" are other examples.

"Instrinsic" rewards, on the other hand, are inherent in the activity itself; the reward is the achievement. They cannot be *directly* controlled externally, although characteristics of the environment can enhance or limit the individual's opportunities to obtain them. Thus, achievement of knowledge or skill, of autonomy, of self-respect, of solutions to problems are examples. So are some of the rewards associated with genuine altruism, giving love and help to others.

Management has rather fully exploited the possibilities of influencing behavior by controlling extrinsic rewards and punishments (although there are some important exceptions which will be considered later). In general, however, far less attention has been given to intrinsic rewards. There are, I believe, two major reasons. The first is the difficulty in establishing a direct linkage between these rewards and performance. One can give money as a promotion for superior performance. The causal linkage is obvious to the recipient, as is the source of the reward. One cannot give a "sense of accomplishment" that accompanies the individual's or group's recognition of having found a solution to a difficult and important problem. (This is quite different from the *extrinsic* reward of praise for the achievement.) The individual can be prevented from obtaining such rewards, for example, by close supervision that gives him no opportunity to solve problems on his own. It is interesting and significant, however, that under such circumstances people will often obtain this reward by ingenious solutions to "problems," which involve a kind of sabotage of management's control system. "Beating the system" is a widely played game in which intrinsic rewards are highly motivational.

The second reason for management's failure to exploit the possibilities of intrinsic rewards is closely associated with beliefs about the nature of man that have been prominent in Western culture for at least two centuries. We need not become involved in the philosophical debate concerning the relationships between mind and body except to recognize that a central issue has been whether man's behavior can be explained in terms of purely mechanical analogies or whether it is necessary to assume the existence of "forces" that may be independent of physical law. However managers have resolved this issue personally, managerial practice appears to reflect at least a tacit belief that motivating people *to work* is a "mechanical" problem.

There are certain similarities between this view of man at work and Newton's Laws of Motion. To a considerable degree, man has been perceived to be like a physical body at rest. It requires the application of external force to set him in motion—to motivate him to work. Consequently, extrinsic rewards and punishments are the obvious and appropriate "forces" to be utilized in controlling organized human effort.

Probably few managers today would accept these assertions as true of their own managerial philosophy. Most would insist that they recognize man to be to some degree "self-activated." They would point particularly to that small proportion of the population that includes the "natural leaders." These men are ambitious by nature; they possess initiative and a desire to assume responsibility; they do not require the application of external force to set them in motion, although of course they do respond to extrinsic rewards.

In addition, it would be argued that even the average man

is self-activated in certain ways. He expends energy in play, in pursuing hobbies, and in other pleasure-seeking activities. Some individuals expend considerable energy, without obvious external cause, in destructive activities that undermine managerial objectives. They are self-motivated, but negatively.

The real point, it would then be argued, is not that man is set in motion only by external forces, but that the internal forces that activate him are—except for "the few"—antithetical to the requirements of organized human effort. He can be directed into productive effort at work only by means of extrinsic rewards and punishment.

Whichever view one takes, then, the outcome in terms of managerial strategy is identical: extrinsic rewards and punishments are the appropriate methods for controlling the behavior of the great majority of human beings.

This is an important issue. If human nature is essentially as thus described, intrinsic rewards and punishments have little or no value for the manager. In fact, a major part of the managerial task is that of counteracting natural human tendencies that are opposed to the goals of organization.

A view that is often expressed by managers today says, "Most people want maximum rewards for minimum effort. They want security—guarantee of employment and protection against most of the hazards of life. They tend to be indifferent or even negative toward reasonable standards of performance." As those managers who hold this view see the situation, these characteristics of human nature are being steadily reinforced by government, labor unions, and some managements that have the unfortunate tendency to be too soft.

If, on the other hand, the self-activated characteristics of man are not *by their nature* antithetical to the requirements of organized human effort, the possibility exists that they could become assets to management rather than liabilities. If some substantial majority of human beings are not prevented *by nature* from being like "the few" (at least in a motivational sense), intrinsic rewards and punishments could be significant tools of management.

It is this view of human nature that is supported by much current behavioral science knowledge. The "mechanical" view is not wrong; it is insufficient to account for a considerable amount of man's behavior at work. A large number of research studies have provided evidence of many ways in which intrinsic rewards can yield higher performance and reduce opposition to organization goals, and of many ways in which intrinsic punishment (often unwittingly imposed by management) can have the opposite consequences.

We will examine some of these findings and their implications for managerial practice in later chapters.[1] One example will serve as an illustration for the moment.

A series of studies in I.B.M. revealed that the introduction of work standards in certain departments by a strategy utilizing extrinsic rewards and punishments brought about increased performance and also lowered morale. In certain other departments, managers opposed to this strategy brought about equivalent improvements *without* negative influences on morale. The essential difference in the latter case was in the utilization of intrinsic rewards associated with the desire of workers to "control their own fate," i.e., to have a greater degree of autonomy than was possible with the *imposition* of standards that was involved in the former case.

These studies did not investigate the negative side effects, other than morale, that have been found typically to be

[1] The reference is to the book Professor McGregor was working on. Plans are being made to publish this book posthumously (Ed.).

associated with the conventional strategies of introducing work standards. In terms of cost and efficiency, these additional side effects (various methods invented by workers for "beating the system") have been frequently demonstrated to be substantial.

A Theory of Motivation

Strictly speaking, the answer to the question managers so often ask of behavioral scientists—"How do you motivate people?"—is, "You don't." Man is by nature motivated. He is an "organic" system, not a mechanical one. Inputs of energy (sunlight, food, water, etc.) are transformed by him into outputs of behavior (including intellectual activities and emotional responses, as well as observable actions). His behavior is influenced by relationships between his characteristics as an organic system (I) and the environment (E). Creating these relationships is a matter of *releasing* his energy in certain ways rather than others. We do not motivate him, because he *is* motivated. When he is not, he is dead. This is the sense in which the behavioral scientist distinguishes between an organic and purely mechanical theory of human nature.

In an earlier volume [2] I attempted to summarize a view of the motivational nature of man associated prominently with the name of Abraham Maslow. This theory has gained considerable support from other behavioral scientists. Its central thesis is that human needs are organized into a hierarchy, with the physical needs for survival at the base. At progressively higher levels are needs for security, social interaction, and ego satisfaction. Generally speaking, when

[2] Douglas McGregor, *The Human Side of Enterprise*. New York: McGraw Hill Book Company, 1960.

lower-level needs are reasonably well satisfied, successively higher levels of needs become relatively more important as motivators of behavior.

The relationships are by no means as simple as this brief statement implies. For example, "reasonable satisfaction" is culturally defined. A subsistence level of satisfaction of physical needs in our society today is far higher than that, say, in the villages of India. Moreover, man's higher-level needs are not completely absent, even at bare subsistence levels. He seeks ways of achieving his social and ego needs, even when he is relatively deprived with respect to his lower needs.

Even in circumstances of severe deprivation, many may rebel against social and political restrictions in the interests of their higher needs. In general, however, the relative strength of human needs is consistent with the hierarchy described above.

Another qualification is that severe deprivation of lower-level needs in early life may warp the individual's adjustment in a variety of ways and accentuate their importance for him permanently (except as psychotherapy may later modify his adjustment). Thus we find people with "fixations" on money, for example, or security, or power.

Man's goals associated with his physical, security, and social needs are achieved largely by means of extrinsic rewards that are controlled by others. It is because of this that mutual trust is such a basic requirement of effective organizational relationships. In its absence there is no assurance to employees of equity in the administration of wages and salaries, promotion, or discipline. In its absence also, management must establish tight controls and exercise close surveillance over employees.

Some of the goals associated with ego needs are achieved

by means of extrinsic rewards—for example, recognition and status. Others, as noted earlier, are achieved solely by intrinsic rewards. The difficulty with intrinsic rewards, from management's point of view, is in utilizing them for purposes of control. I have argued above that part of the problem lies in the mistaken assumption that these needs are by their nature antithetical to the purposes of the industrial organization—that they are expressed in pleasure-seeking activities and not through work. Let us examine this assumption further.

If the expenditure of energy is work, it is clear that human beings often work hard at their hobbies and in other pleasureful activities. They work hard in acquiring skills or knowledge that they wish to acquire. They work hard in the service of "causes" to which they are committed—in civic or political or religious or social or humanitarian organizations. They expend energy in organized artistic activities: musical or theatrical or graphic art organizations.

It is often argued that most people are by nature dependent—that they prefer not to accept responsibility but to be led. If we observe their behavior on the job, the generalization appears to hold. Yet it is surprising how many of these same people not only accept but seek responsibility in a variety of organized activities away from the job.

Intrinsic rewards are significant in all these activities, although extrinsic rewards (status, recognition, social acceptance) are involved as well. The basic point is that intrinsic rewards are not associated exclusively with human activities of the kind that are defined as recreational. Nor are such activities carried on exclusively outside of organizational settings. It is not human nature that excludes the pursuit of goals yielding intrinsic rewards from the job environment. It is not human nature that defines pleasure-seeking activities as nonproductive. Human needs can be satisfied in a great variety of environments. With the exception of a very few (such as sleep and sex), they can be satisfied through activities that management would define as productive, as well as through activities that management would define otherwise.

It is my belief that a realistic perception of man in these respects has been obscured in our culture for a very long time by the moral conviction that pleasure is sinful and must therefore be dissociated from productive work. To earn his daily bread by the sweat of his brow is the punishment meted out to man ever since Adam and Eve were driven out from the Garden; it is through painful and unpleasant effort that man atones for his sins and develops strength of character; what is good cannot be obtained through pleasureful activity. Certainly this is not the full explanation, but the influence of this social norm in our society is strong and pervasive.

The motivational theory under discussion asserts that man —if he is freed to some extent, by his presence in an affluent society, from the necessity to use most of his energy to obtain the necessities of life and a degree of security from the major vicissitudes—will by nature begin to pursue goals associated with his higher-level needs. These include needs for a degree of control over his own fate, for self-respect, for using and increasing his talents, for responsibility, for achievement both in the sense of status and recognition and in the sense of personal development and effective problem solving. Thus freed, he will also seek in many ways to satisfy more fully his physical needs for recreation, relaxation, and play. Management has been well aware of the latter tendency; it has not often recognized the former, or at least it has not taken into account its implications for managerial strategy.

A statement of strategy that has long seemed to me to be consistent with the goals of economic enterprise on the one hand, and with behavioral science knowledge of the motivational nature of man on the other, is this: to seek to create conditions (an organizational environment) such that members of the organization at all levels can best achieve their own goals by directing their efforts toward the goals of the organization. With respect to lower-level needs, this places before management the task of providing extrinsic rewards, *on an equitable basis*, for all kinds of contributions to the success of the enterprise. Since management controls these rewards, and can therefore both give and withhold them, this task also involves the equitable administration of extrinsic punishment for "negative" contributions. Note that this statement is careful not to relate these rewards and punishments to compliance or noncompliance with management's wishes. It cannot be assumed—in fact, it is often untrue—that a given manager's wishes are the expression of the goals of the enterprise (even sometimes when he is a top-level executive).

With respect to higher-level ego needs (and some middle-level social needs), management's task is to provide opportunities for members of the organization to obtain *intrinsic* rewards from contributions to the success of the enterprise. Since management does not directly control such rewards, the problem of equity in their administration does not arise. The task is to provide an appropriate environment —one that will permit and encourage employees to seek intrinsic rewards *at work*. Its performance will involve managers at every level in an examination of the way work is organized, the nature and administration of managerial controls, the way responsibilities are assigned and supervised, the way goals are set, policies established, planning is done— in short, in almost every aspect of managerial practice. Often the provision of opportunities for intrinsic rewards becomes a matter of removing restraints. Progress is rarely fast, because people who have become accustomed to control through extrinsic rewards exclusively must learn new attitudes and habits before they can feel secure in accepting opportunities for intrinsic rewards at work. If there is not a fair degree of mutual trust, and some positive support, the whole idea may appear highly risky.

It will not be fruitful for management to undertake this task unless there is genuine open-mindedness (if not acceptance) with respect to the motivational character of human nature outlined in the preceding page.

In one area of industrial organizations—namely, the scientific research laboratory involved primarily in basic research—management has generally gone a considerable way toward accomplishing this task. The reasons for doing so have been largely connected with the problem of obtaining and keeping competent scientists, rather than with the acceptance of ideas like those given above concerning human nature. (In fact, I have heard many managers assert vehemently that scientists are not at all representative of *homo sapiens!*) I doubt that these results would have been achieved except for the external pressures that have almost literally forced changes in policy and practice on some of these managements. Those pressures are not evident to anything like the same degree in the rest of the industrial organizations today.

One of the generalizations that emerges from these considerations about motivation and human nature is this: when a manager asserts, on the basis of his experience and observation, that most people are by nature either indifferent or antagonistic toward the goals of the industrial enterprise, there is more than a small possibility that he may be confusing cause and effect. The indifference and hostility often are observable, but they may be the *result* of a managerial strategy that has, over a long period, provided adequate extrinsic rewards for lower-level needs but has ignored or even prevented the achievement of intrinsic rewards associated with higher-level needs. The former needs, being reasonably well satisfied, have become less motivational; the latter, being frustrated, are finding expression outside the organization (and perhaps also in the exercise of ingenuity to "beat the system" inside the organization).

Another generalization emerging from an organic conception of human nature is that all human relationships are "transactional." Since the normal individual is not passive toward his environment, but is actively "coping" with it, influence in any form is a two-way process.

Raymond Bauer,[3] in a penetrating analysis of research on social communication, shows how behavioral scientists have gradually come to recognize that even communication via mass media ("obviously" a one-way form of influence) is transactional in significant ways. The reciprocal influence in social communication is not necessarily balanced—there may be inequities either way. The point is that it is never fully one way.

The reactions of the "influenced" may not be directly or immediately observable to the "influencer," but this does not mean that they are absent. The manager whose conception of cause and effect in human behavior is mechanical must rely on the "orneriness" of human nature for an explanation of the many indifferences or resistances to managerial in-

[3] "The Obstinate Audience. The Influence Process from the Point of View of Social Communication." *American Psychologist*, 1964, *19*, 319–328.

fluence. The only way he can conceive of to counteract them is to increase the threat of extrinsic punishment (which often aggravates the symptoms he is trying to eliminate).

The manager whose conception of cause and effect is organic will recognize the transactional character of influence. When he encounters indifference or resistance, he will not attribute the reaction to human nature, but to aspects of the relationship between E and I variables which can be analyzed and probably corrected by *cooperative* interaction.

The values in "participation" as a tactic of management do not lie merely, or even primarily, in the fact that "people like to be consulted" about decisions affecting them. It is that participation, when it is sincere and genuine, is an open recognition of the interactional character of influence. When resistance to or sabotage of managerial decisions is anticipated, participation provides a natural method for minimizing or eliminating them in advance.

Thus a manager's view of human nature powerfully influences his selection of a strategy. His strategy in turn powerfully influences the behavior of his subordinates. Naturally, he takes the evidence provided by their behavior as proof of his views of human nature. Such circular reactions can occur with incorrect or inadequate beliefs about human nature as well as with adequate ones. Once they are established, contrary evidence is often rejected on the ground that it is inconsistent with directly observable reality.

Such situations are by no means limited to management or to the behavioral sciences. They have been repeated countless times throughout history in the physical sciences, as man has rejected evidence contradicting his direct experience of reality. It is often decades, and sometimes centuries, before these issues are finally resolved.

I can assert no more, then, than that the evidence from

the behavioral science, as I and some, but not all, of my colleagues interpret it, affirms this conception of the motivational dynamics of human nature.

Perceived Versus Objective Reality

Another important property of human nature has been elaborated as a result of behavioral science research. It is that human behavior is seldom a *direct* response to objective reality, but is rather a response to the individual's perception of that reality. A simple reflex, such as the removal of the finger from the hot stove, appears to be a direct response to reality. But even it is mediated by the nervous system. Impulses must flow in through sensory nerves and back out through nerves controlling muscular action before the response can occur. Moreover, as a result of learning, the individual may on occasion refrain from touching a stove in the belief that it is hot when in fact it is not. He responds to *his perception* of reality.

Human response to more complex aspects of reality involve higher levels of the nervous system, which have certain important characteristics. Among the most important of these are the processes of selective perception and memory by which the individual organizes his perception of reality.

We recognize these processes readily enough in some circumstances. A common expression is: "That's not the way I see it." However, we tend to think of this phenomenon as being restricted to ambiguous situations such as those associated with politics or broad social issues. It is not easy to accept the fact that even our perceptions of relatively simple aspects of physical reality are mediated by the selectivity of perception, by our capacity to see what we expect to see, by the cosmology we have developed about the nature of the world, and by our needs and wishes or our fears and anxieties. It is to a large extent our perception of reality, not reality itself, that influences and determines our behavior.

Consider the behavior of man as it was influenced until the end of the fifteenth century by his perception of a flat rather than spherical earth. Consider the differences in behavior between a doctor and a layman who might undertake to treat the layman's illness. The layman has the disease. Nevertheless, his perception of reality would in many instances lead him to adopt a method of treatment quite different from what the doctor would prescribe on the basis of his own more professional perception. Consider the question of equity with respect to the administration of salaries or promotions and the quite different perceptions of management and of workers concerning reality. The effort, time, and money devoted to the development of an appropriate "corporate image" by some companies today is at least a tacit admission that man responds not to reality directly but to his perception of it.

This basic point about cause and effect in human behavior is central to this argument. It requires emphasis because it is one of the "facts of life" that we as human beings find most difficult to accept, even though we have continuous evidence of it in our own behavior and in the behavior of others.

Rational Versus Emotional Man

Another important aspect of the nature of human nature from the managerial point of view has to do with the emotional characteristics of behavior and their control. The thoughtful manager today is relatively well informed concerning at least some of these characteristics of human nature. He accepts the fact that some are unconscious and thus uncontrollable by the individual. He is aware of the general findings in psychosomatic medicine and clinical psychology.

Many managers act, however, as though they believe that man is divisible into two *separate* individuals, (1) a rational person who can operate logically, deal with facts, and reach purely objective conclusions, and (2) an emotional person who is blindly irrational, ignores or misinterprets facts, and operates in a highly biased fashion. Managers, of course, desire to deal with the former "person" and to exclude the influence of the latter. The ability to make the separation, it is assumed, rests in part on the individual's education and intellectual skills, but primarily on the exercise of will power and the conscious intention to be rational. This ability is believed to be particularly characteristic of "the few."

Thus, the tacit belief, reflected in much managerial behavior, is that at least some men can become, if they choose, rational, logical, decision-making machines, with respect to business problems. Verbal persuasion is usually applied to make man into this kind of a machine: "Let's keep personalities out of this"; "Let's deal with the facts"; "Consider the problems coldly and objectively." If man can be persuaded to do so, he can largely eliminate the influences on his thinking or behavior of his needs, fears, wishes, anxieties, hostilities, and guilts.

Behavioral science challenges sharply this conception of the nature of man. The evidence from the psychological clinic and from a considerable body of experimental research is conclusive. Except possibly for the most trivial acts, man's behavior—whether he is thinking, analyzing, reasoning, or interacting with others—is *always* influenced significantly by emotional factors, some conscious and some unconscious. The more important the problem or issue under consideration is for him, the greater the influence of emotional factors on his responses. Others cannot eliminate these influences by the giving of orders or the making of requests, nor can he eliminate them by the conscious willful effort to do so. The emotional and the rational aspects of man are inextricably interwoven and only to a very slight degree separable.

A careful study of performance reviews in a division of a large manufacturing company led to a conclusion consistent with these generalizations. It is virtually impossible within the content of the conventional appraisal interview for a superior to communicate a negative evaluation of a subordinate's performance to him without producing defensive reactions. The more severe the criticism (as perceived by the subordinate), the more the defensiveness. Thus, the subordinate does not react rationally to "the facts." He fails to hear them, or he misinterprets them, or he rejects them as untrue. Much as he may wish to do so, he cannot in these circumstances turn himself into a rational machine. In consequence, the changes in behavior attributable to requests by superiors in the content of the appraisal interview turned out in this study to be few indeed.

Human beings in relationships that involve differences in power and status are particularly vulnerable to the effects of emotional forces. The highly sensitive nature of these relationships in childhood and adolescence creates lasting tendencies to react emotionally as well as rationally to them. There are, for example, always subtle and sometimes obvious changes in a subordinate's behavior when he deals directly with those above him in the managerial hierarchy.

Such control as the individual may gain over emotional factors influencing his own behavior appears to rest heavily on the degree to which he can accept his feelings as facts. If he can come to recognize them, to understand something of the circumstances that aroused them, to accept them as inevitable and integral aspects of his behavior, he can reduce to some extent their effects on his rational behavior.

When a manager is dealing with his subordinates, their feelings are part of "the facts" whatever the matter under consideration may be. The ability to deal effectively with any problem is lessened to the degree that such feelings are suppressed. A good decision can only be made when all the relevant facts are available. To attempt to exclude emotional facts when dealing with subordinates (or peers, or superiors) on any managerial matter is to rely on a kind of primitive magic: the belief that important and often controlling aspects of reality can be eliminated by the performance of rituals or the pronouncement of incantations.

It is perhaps not too difficult for the manager to give lip service to these feelings about the emotional nature of man. Many do. To include them genuinely in his view of reality so that they become part of the basis for his actions is another matter. The manager is also an example of rational-emotional human nature. His own feelings—partly conscious and partly unconscious—exert important influence on his ability to accept fully that man is not separable into a rational being and an emotional man. To accept the implications of the fact would, for example, alter considerably his view of what is predictable and controllable in the organizational reality that surrounds him.

An important aspect of the lives of 45 to 50 Sloan Fellows during the year they spend at M.I.T. in the Management Program is the organization of their own social activities. Since their families move with them to the Boston area for the year, and since they are quite different as a group from the other students at M.I.T., they tend to do many things together.

The management of their extracurricular activities is entirely up to the group. Experience indicates that, if they leave these matters to chance, they are likely to lose kinds of control that most of them consider important. They become "managed" by the implicit norms and standards that develop in any organization unless explicit attention is given to them.

These matters received rather full discussion in the initial phases of the program for a recent group of Sloan Fellows. The discussion took place in subgroups of a dozen men each. Afterward, in a general session, the suggestion was made and adopted that each subgroup select two representatives to meet together to explore these issues further, preparatory to dealing with them formally. The subgroups then met to select their representatives.

In one group, which I observed, there were clearly different feelings about the issues involved and about the task of choosing representatives. These, however, were ignored and the suggestion of one member that they select their representative by secret ballot was immediately accepted. Then the suggestion was made that people might feel quite differently about the importance of this problem, that some would welcome the opportunity to serve as representatives whereas others would resent being chosen. The group then encouraged individual members to express their feelings. Because the power relationships were negligible (the group consisted of peers), several members did so. It became apparent that, out of twelve, about six felt that the issues were trivial, that they had more important things to do and would therefore much prefer not to be chosen. Two or three others were relatively neutral and would serve willingly if asked. Three, for various reasons, expressed interest in the issues and a genuine desire to have the opportunity to join the "task force."

With this knowledge, the group then proceeded to the secret ballot. Two of the three who had expressed a desire to serve were elected.

This was not a critical managerial decision, obviously. The consideration of emotional factors, however, influenced the result materially. What impressed me was that, if the issue had been a genuinely important one, there would have been a far greater likelihood that feelings would have been denied, ignored, or suppressed in the making of the decision. In this particular case, the implementation of the decision (the work of the task force) might not have been materially affected by the presence of representatives who disliked the task. If the issue had been important, it is not hard to imagine that the implementation desired would have been far less than optimal.

Some of my academic colleagues are fond of saying that emotion is a dirty word in management's lexicon. This is a pointed and largely accurate description. A less colorful but equally correct statement is that management appears to want to eliminate the effects of emotion on behavior in the organizational setting. The evidence of behavioral science indicates, on the contrary, that, to the extent that this objective was achieved, the organization would reduce its ability to survive!

The essential difficulty is that the typical managerial view of emotion is highly restricted. Human loyalty, enthusiasm, drive, commitment, acceptance of responsibility, and self-confidence are all emotional variables. So are all the values "we hold dear." Motivation is an *emotional* force.

Moreover, the evidence grows that intellectual creativity (as well as artistic creativity) is a process involving emotional factors. Clearly, management does not desire to eliminate these characteristics of human nature from its own or its employees' behavior. In fact, if a human being existed who was completely unemotional, objective, and logical, he would by definition have no *interest* in the success of any organization. He would not be motivated.

The real desire of the manager is that human beings (particularly those with whom he must interact) should express certain emotions and suppress others. He would like to eliminate such emotional characteristics as antagonism, hostility, resistance, defiance, uncooperative attitudes, and "unrealistic" points of view. He would like to eliminate emotional forces that are associated in his mind with "bad," "selfish," "immature," "unreasonable" behavior. (In fact, many of these forces are unconscious and, therefore, are precisely those that cannot be eliminated by conscious intent.)

There is also a cultural factor involved in these implicit desires. The model of the successful manager in our culture is a masculine one. The good manager is aggressive, competitive, firm, just. He is not feminine; he is not soft, or yielding, or dependent, or intuitive in the womanly sense. The very expression of emotion is widely viewed as a "feminine weakness" that would interfere with effective business processes. Yet, the fact is that these emotions are part of the human nature of men and women alike. Cultural forces have shaped not their existence but their acceptability; they are repressed, *but this does not make them inactive.* They continue to influence attitudes, opinions, and decisions.

There is solid physiological evidence of the existence in man of a two-part nervous system, the central and the "autonomic." Very roughly, these can be identified with intellectual and emotional activities. They are highly interdependent. Changes in one subsystem affect the other and therefore the total system. In fact, physiological evidence is that man would die without the contribution of his autonomic nervous system which, in addition to its influence on emotional expression, regulates critical bodily functions such as the heartbeat. It is therefore self-defeating to managerial purposes, as well as physically impossible, to accept a cosmology in which human emotion is relegated to an undesirable role.

To what degree can the individual control the effects of emotional influence on his rationality? If one accepts the evidence of clinical psychology, the answer is, "not very much." The "public" *expression* of emotion—anger or anxiety, for example—can be consciously suppressed. In addition, some emotional factors in every individual's past experience are *repressed*, that is to say, they have been banished from consciousness, and the individual is completely unaware of their existence. In either case, however, emotional influences affect behavior whenever they are aroused. The observable external clues may be very slight: flushing, tenseness, irritability, unusual passivity or quietness, and so forth.

It can be stated with some assurance that emotions will influence behavior, including thinking, reasoning, and decision making, whenever they are aroused. Second, they will be aroused to the degree that the issue or problem is important. Third, importance is a function of the (conscious or unconscious) meaning of the issue or the problem or the situation *to the individual*. We acquire the ability to predict with fair accuracy unique stimuli that arouse emotion—however well hidden—in individuals whom we know well.

It is of course possible for objective reality to be so coercive that the effects of emotional factors upon behavior become negligible, at least for the moment. Thus "the facts" can determine a decision completely, although the subsequent implementation of the decision may be substantially affected positively or negatively by emotional influences. It is rare, however, for a managerial decision of more than trivial significance to be completely determined by the facts. Even when the facts appear to be coercive, there is usually room for doubt concerning their interpretation or their veracity. Scientific findings are the subject of frequent and sometimes bitter dispute on this score, despite the elaborate safeguards characteristic of scientific methods.

Complete objectivity is a rare phenomenon unless the issues are of little consequence to the individual. This is not to deny the possibility of some gain in striving for it. It is rather to assert that it cannot be achieved in oneself merely by conscious intent, or in others by command. To believe otherwise is to put one's faith in magic.

One of the strong arguments for the value of group problem solving and group decision making when complex and important issues are involved is that human beings have a greater capacity to perceive emotion in others than in themselves. In a group setting—provided the expression of feelings as well as of ideas and opinions is not taboo—members can help each other recognize and make allowances for emotional influences and thus reduce their impact. This means of improving objectivity can be utilized successfully only under certain conditions. Greater objectivity is not a simple, automatic consequence of bringing individuals together to make decisions or solve problems.

The general implication from behavioral science is that man is by nature an inseparable mixture of rational and emotional components. He cannot turn himself into a rational "machine" by any known means, nor can he eliminate the effects of emotion on intellectual activity in others by persuasion or by command.

Social Man

It is hardly necessary to call attention to the degree to which our society stresses the values of individualism. We have done so for three and a half centuries. Negative attitudes toward conformity, dislike of being "other-directed," carefully contrived legal protection of individual rights, certain attitudes toward government, all reflect these values. The manager, as a member of our society, tends to share them. Thus he stresses strongly the desirability of dealing with individuals as he carries out his managerial responsibilities.

Of course he cannot permit complete individual freedom. A degree of standardization of behavior is obviously necessary. Otherwise there would be no such thing as organizations. In general, his cosmology includes a view of the individual as the appropriate unit of organization. As a consequence, he tends to respond negatively to what he is likely to perceive as "collectivization," whether in the form of face-to-face work groups or in the form of a union. Oddly, he does not frown on "teamwork"; he does not perceive the team as a "collective."

Of course, this view of reality has its emotional aspects, whether or not they are recognized. The manager's power may be appreciably affected, depending on whether he deals with individuals or groups.

In many cases, the manager's cosmology includes the view that a group is an inefficient means for getting work done, particularly when it comes to activities like planning, decision making, innovating, problem solving. It is in the nature of human nature, as he views it, that intellectual activities in particular are individual activities, which are impaired by being carried on in a group.

There is much in experience and everyday observation to support this belief. By and large, groups, committees, and task forces *are* grossly inefficient in these respects. Again, however, the question arises as to whether these are *inherent* characteristics of group activity—unchangeable human nature—or whether they are the *result* of the way groups are managed.

In the last few years, there has been some change in this aspect of managerial cosmology. Formal educative processes designed to improve understanding and skill with respect to group activity have had an impact. The controversy concerning the individual versus the group is by no means settled, but the complexity of reality in a modern industrial organization is gradually producing a reluctant acceptance that groups are appropriate for some kinds of managerial activity. Nevertheless, fundamentally most managers perceive human nature in terms of individual nature. Individual man is the proper organizational unit.

The evidence from the behavioral science indicates clearly that the human being is a social organism. Whether he is inherently so may be debatable, but from birth on he lives and seeks many of his goals in groups. In fact, at birth and for sometime thereafter, his successful survival depends on his being a member of a group. The universality of the family is not an accident of human history.

One would expect to find a substantial carry-over from early experiences in groups to other aspects of man's life, including his employment in industrial organizations, and this is of course what we do find. The classic studies of the Harvard group at the Hawthorne Works of the Western Electric Company in the 1920's are a major case in point. The studies of William Foote Whyte on incentive systems, the evidence accumulated by the Institute for Social Research at the University of Michigan, the work of Kurt Lewin and his successors, and much else have served to extend and refine knowledge about group behavior.

A number of extrinsic rewards and punishments, as well as intrinsic ones, are associated with man's social needs. These needs include not only those for acceptance, support, and recognition in group settings, but also the need to give these rewards to fellow members. In this case the rewards are inherent in the action; they are intrinsic. Under appropriate conditions, the group can also be a setting within which the individual satisfies many of his most important ego needs, including those for learning, autonomy (despite a common belief to the contrary), leadership, and self-fulfillment. A view of reality that ignores or denies these possibilities for goal achievement, or that sees them as inherently incompatible with organizational objectives and requirements, is greatly limited with respect to the managerial task of "motivating people to work."

It is important to recognize that the growth of behavioral science's knowledge about groups has not resulted in the conclusion that it is necessary to *choose* between the individual and the group. Just as in the physical sciences, understanding of the phenomena at different levels is necessary for production control. The physical particle exhibits properties that are replicated in the atom, in the molecule, and even in a planetary system. However, there are also properties that are unique to each level, and our ability to control natural phenomena is increased by knowledge of the properties of physical systems at different levels.

Similarly with human behavior. We study characteristics of cells, of organs, of the nervous system as a whole, of the human being as an organism, of groups, and of larger organizations of human beings. Certain characteristics are common to all these "systems," others are unique to each level. Management's insistence that the individual is the unit of organization is as limiting as would be an engineer's insistence that the molecule is *the* unit of physical systems. The limitations of a physical technology based on knowledge of one level alone would be great indeed.

A molecule is an assembly of atoms, to be sure, but certain

relationships among the atoms result in molecules with given properties, whereas other relationships result in molecules with entirely different properties. These properties of molecules cannot be predicted solely on the basis of knowledge of the properties of the individual atoms.

Considerations of a similar nature lead the behavioral scientist to question many managerial assertions about the inherent characteristics of human groups. These assertions are based almost entirely on attempts to deal with groups in terms of knowledge of individual behavior. The accumulated behavioral science knowledge about *group* behavior tends to contradict the idea that the properties of groups are inherently or inevitably those that we typically observe when we deal with groups as mere collections of individuals.

It is demonstrably possible to create relationships between individuals that make up a face-to-face group such that the group exhibits properties almost diametrically opposed to those observed in the typical committee or staff group or task force in everyday organizational life.

Such groups make decisions that are effectively implemented, they are creative and innovative, they operate efficiently, they are not crippled by disagreements nor hampered by dominant personalities. Pressures for conformity are minimal, the knowledge and skills of each member are effectively utilized. The "outputs" of the group need not be mediocre or least-common-denominator compromises, but can often yield decisions and solutions at a level of performance superior to the sum of the outputs of the individual members operating separately. Finally, the members see the group as a setting within which there are attractive opportunities to achieve many of their individual goals and to gain intrinsic rewards.

The characteristics of such effective groups will be considered in later chapters, as well as some practical considerations about their development. For the moment, the essential point is that a managerial cosmology limited to "man the individual" excludes important possibilities of improved organizational effectiveness.

Summary

The manager's view of reality is, of course, far wider and more complex than this discussion would suggest. It includes his view of the physical world and, at a deeper level, his beliefs, however implicit, concerning "the meaning of it all."

The function of a cosmology is to bring some semblance of order into experiences that otherwise would be so confusing that there would be no basis for action. It is difficult to imagine the anxiety that would result if man had no conception of cause and effect, no way of ordering his perception of reality and his experience with it. Thus, a cosmology is importantly associated with the individual's basic security, his confidence that he can cope successfully with physical and social reality.

The individual never experiences a complete lack of order in reality (except perhaps in early childhood), because he is endowed with a nervous system that enables him to perceive and remember selectively, to generalize, to relate, to discriminate. Inevitably, he develops strong needs to find order in complexity. In fact, his needs frequently lead him to impose order on reality even when it is not objectively "there." His possession of these characteristics, plus the fact that he lives in a culture in which there are already existing ordered views of reality, provides him with the basis for developing a cosmology.

In some sense every individual's cosmology is unique. In other respects all individuals share common beliefs about reality. However, no cosmology *is* reality; it is a human perception of reality. It is like a map of a territory that has been only partly explored and perhaps never will be completely known. The traveler therefore must rely to some extent on his own wits, using his map but remembering always that it is an imperfect representation of reality.

I have tried to indicate a few ways in which the accumulating behavioral science knowledge has changed the map upon which the managerial traveler in our society has tended to rely. But my analogy appears to break down, because some of this knowledge contradicts the direct evidence provided by the manager's experience. He finds that the map does not correspond with his direct observation of the territory through which he is traveling. This is not, however, an unusual circumstance.

As indicated earlier, all of us have come to terms in some fashion with findings in *physical* science that contradict our direct experience. Such knowledge asserts that the sun and planets do not rise and set as they appear to do, that ordinary physical objects are in fact not solid as they seem to be, that invisible and unexperienced biological organisms affect our health and well-being, that what appear to be simple cause-effect relationships are in fact extremely complex.

Similarly, behavioral science knowledge involves assertions about the nature of man and of cause and effect in human behavior that challenge direct experience. Some of these findings are backed by sufficient research so that one can have considerable confidence that they are true. Some are still subject to controversy; like all scientific knowledge, they represent partial truth, and there may be material changes as new knowledge accumulates.

The manager's view of reality exerts profound effects upon his every managerial act. His acts in turn affect both the achievement of his own goals and those of the organization of which he is a member. If he is concerned with how well these goals are achieved, he cannot afford to be indifferent to the implications of the findings of behavioral science.

The Manager's View of Organization

One map upon which managers have relied for many years is the organization chart and its associated set of position descriptions. This map represents the organization as a structure of responsibilities and a structure of authority. The logic for viewing organizational reality this way is persuasive, and the tendency, therefore, has been to accept this map as a good representation of reality.

The familiar view is that, in a small company, the president (who may also be the owner) carries on all managerial functions. With growth of the firm, some division of labor becomes necessary. Consequently, the president hires other managers to whom he assigns responsibilities for certain parts of the total function. However, in doing so, he retains the over-all responsibility for the organization, even though he no longer carries on all the managerial activities.

As the organization grows, each of these subdivisions of responsibility may be further divided, but with the same conception that each manager retains responsibility for everything that is assigned to him from above. Each managerial position on the chart thus depicts what a man is responsible for, although not necessarily what he does.

Such subdivisions may take many forms. Thus, we have maps of organizations that are functional, or that are organized by product or geographically, or that are organized in terms of some combination of these. We have divisions and departments and smaller work units. One favored conception today is that of the "profit center," in which most if not all of the managerial functions for a given product or group of products are assigned to a unit headed by a man who is himself much like the president of a small organization, and who is responsible for the financial profitability of his "center."

In order to ensure the fulfillment of these responsibilities and to enable coordination of the parts, there is a structure of authority. The manager of each part, beginning with the smallest, is responsible to the manager of the next larger part, but he has authority within defined limits over his subdivision. From the top down, therefore, one has a chain of command; in order to keep responsibilities clear, each man must have one boss to whom he is directly responsible and who has authority over him.

Some functional divisions are designed to provide help, advice, and service to the line organization. Managers of such functions have authority only within their functions. However, the head of each such function is again responsible to one boss in the line organization. There are many variations on this aspect of the map, and certain qualifications are sometimes felt to be necessary. For example, a staff manager in a subdivision of a major organization may report "functionally" to the staff manager at headquarters, but "operationally" to the manager of the subdivision.

Since it seems obvious that a man cannot fulfill his responsibilities effectively if he has too many people reporting directly to him, the concept of span of control is invoked. When the number of subordinates reporting directly to a given manager is felt to be unreasonably large, the organization is modified by creating additional levels of subdivisions as necessary.

Thus, we have a map of the organization, constructed from a series of positions, which defines a structure of responsibility and a structure of authority. In addition, the necessary policies and procedures are formulated to define the interrelationships involved. This map is essentially static, in that it is conceived to be changed only by a formal reorganization of these relationships. Minor adjustments to individual positions, of course, can and do occur without reorganization.

The thoughtful manager recognizes today that this map is only a very rough approximation of reality at best. It is a formal picture of the organization, of the way things are supposed to be. It is important for resolving conflicts, issuing orders, evaluating performance. However, it is obvious that managerial activities do not coincide completely with the map. There are many ways of getting things done outside the formal channels of organization, and these are used regularly.

It is also obvious that, despite the logical requirement for it, authority never in fact fully equals responsibility. The manager at any level of the organization is held accountable for things that he cannot directly control, even if he has the formal right to do so. Further, it is clear that staff people do more than merely give advice and help, that they exert powerful influences amounting to authority, although not defined as such. Nevertheless, the position descriptions, and the associated policies do give a kind of order to a reality that would otherwise be too complex to grasp.

Some managers, most often in smaller organizations, resist the idea of the formal organization chart. What one usually finds, however, is resistance to its *public* use. There may be a chart, kept in the president's desk, often known about but seldom seem by others.

Many reasons are given for keeping the map of the organization private. Among them is the belief that it may serve to limit too much the acceptance of responsibility at various levels. Managers will protect themselves by staying safely within their own limits. Another argument is that such a formal chart may promote quarrels between managers, or may permit important responsibilities to "fall down the cracks" between the defined limits. Thus, the formal chart is felt to promote bureaucratic rigidity rather than flexibility.

Although these reasons have some truth without a doubt, there are other reasons, less often expressed, that may also play a part. A formal organization chart and its accompanying position descriptions clearly limit the power of the manager in the sense that he cannot be arbitrary in the demands that he makes on his subordinates. His freedom is restricted, and the ease of changing the organization is likewise restricted. The belief also exists that people will work harder if they are uncertain about what is expected of them, and that competitions in a somewhat uncertain situation will in the end enable the best men to survive. Thus the phrase: "Let them work it out among themselves." This conception is essentially the Darwinian one of struggle for survival. It is not surprising that the associated idea that the management organization is a "jungle" often accompanies such a view of reality.

A Systems View of Organization

It was argued earlier that the difficulty with traditional managerial views of cause and effect is not that they are wrong, but that they are too limited. A similar problem exists with the more traditional views concerning the nature of the organization. It becomes necessary with such a conception to consider all the behavior that is unexplained by the "map" as exceptional behavior. This creates a difficulty because what is not explained turns out to be greater than what is.

There are other ways of describing organizations. A common one is to view them in terms of a pattern of communications or "flows" of information. There is a growing tendency today to describe human organizations within a broad framework of thinking that is called "general systems theory." This theory uses certain common concepts to gain understanding of a wide range of phenomena in the physical sciences, in biology, and now in the behavioral sciences. These phenomena are common to different "systems," ranging from the atom to the galaxy, from the cell to the organism, from the individual to society. Let us consider what it means to view an industrial organization as a system within this framework.

A system is an assembly of interdependent parts (subsystems) *whose interaction determines its survival*. Interdependence means that a change in one part affects other parts and thus the whole system. Such a statement is true of atoms, molecules, cells, people, plants, formal organizations, and planetary systems.

The choice of subsystems and of the most strategic unit is to some degree a matter of convenience. In physics, for example, the particle may be the appropriate unit for some purposes, whereas the atom or the molecule may be appropriate for other purposes. One could, in fact, consider an industrial organization as an assembly of molecules, for it is! In our present state of knowledge, this would not be particularly useful. For practical purposes then, the unit that is viewed as basic to the human organization is the individual.

As noted earlier, subsystems at all levels of a major system have properties or characteristics in common. It is also true that each level has certain unique properties. In fact, this is a criterion for selecting appropriate levels. This is an important consideration, for it means that we may usefully expect to find that the individual human organism, the face-to-face work group, the functional department, the division, and the total organization have unique properties as well as properties in common. It is demonstrable that the behavior of the whole (at any level) cannot be fully predicted solely by knowledge of the behavior of its subparts.

An industrial organization is an "open" system. It engages in "transactions" with a larger system, society. There are inputs in the form of people, materials, money, and in the form of political and economic forces arising in the larger system. There are outputs in the form of products, services, and rewards to its members. Similarly, the subsystems within the organization down to the individual are open systems.

An industrial organization is an "organic" system. It is adaptive in the sense that it changes its nature as a result of changes in the external system surrounding it. The adaptation is not passive; the system affects the larger system as well as being affected by it. It "copes" with its environment as the individual human being copes with his. It is dynamic in the sense that it undergoes constant change as a result of the interaction among the subsystems and with the larger environmental system.

Finally, an industrial organization is a "sociotechnical"

system. It is not a mere assembly of buildings, manpower, money, machines, and processes.

The system consists in the *organization* of people around various work "technologies." This means, among other things, that human relations are not an optional feature of an organization; they are a built-in property. The system exists by virtue of the motivated behavior of people. Their relationships and behavior determine the inputs, the transformations, and the outputs of the system.

Thus, an industrial organization, viewed within this framework, is an open, organic, sociotechnical system.

This way of thinking about an organization has several advantages. One of the major ones is that it can represent reality more fully and more adequately than the conventional picture of the formal organization. It provides a better basis for understanding what does go on rather than what ought to go on. It brings the activities of the informal organization into the framework, without excluding those of the formal organization. It enlarges and enriches the possibility of understanding the many complex cause-and-effect relationships that an organization comprises. Thus it promises better prediction and better control. Without becoming highly technical, it is useful to use this systems way of thinking in the examination of many typical organizational phenomena.

14

Why Not Exploit Behavioral Science?

A LARGE SEGMENT of human activity today consists in attempts to influence or control the behavior of other people. The complexity as well as the frequency and spread of human interaction throughout the world has increased immensely during the past century, and with this has come a corresponding increase in efforts to influence others in order to achieve our goals or to prevent interference with their achievement. The pervasive character of influence is apparent throughout every aspect of life, from child-rearing practices in the family to the conduct of the cold war.

Few people would be prepared to argue that the methods currently employed in influencing behavior (attitudes, beliefs, ideas, opinions, as well as actions are included in this term) are adequate to the problems we face. To be sure, we are not unsuccessful. We are able to keep our society from disintegrating into chaos. We create and maintain in-

Based on a talk given at a convocation of alumni of the Sloan Fellowship and the Senior Executive Programs of the Massachusetts Institute of Technology in May 1962.

stitutions—familial, educational, economic, political, cultural —which serve us fairly well most of the time.

However, our accomplishments are generally modest compared to our aspirations, and our failures are impressive. We are dismayed by the incidence of divorce, poverty, delinquency, crime, social conflict, international tension, and war. Moreover, the negative "side effects" of many induced behavior changes are often as difficult to cope with as the original problem. Consider the consequences within our country of devoting 60 per cent of our national budget to a strategy of military deterrence in order to influence the behavior of the Soviet bloc. Or, as a single example among many at the level of everyday organizational life, consider the amount of human ingenuity exercised to *defeat* the control procedures upon which administrators and managers (and educators, and parents, and tax collectors!) rely to control behavior.[1]

We can, if we choose, greatly accelerate the rate at which our ability is increasing to influence, control, change human behavior. The prime requirement for such an accomplishment is the recognition and acceptance of a conception of cause and effect in human behavior that is more realistic than the one we hold almost universally today. The present conception limits us to a very few simple strategies of control; it prevents us from perceiving more effective strategies and a wide array of tactics that are potentially available. We are bound within narrow limits of action by a grossly oversimplified view of the causes of human behavior.

This sounds like a brash contention. Perhaps I may be permitted to present the rationale behind it and a few illustra-

[1] William F. Whyte, *Money and Motivation.* New York: Harper and Brothers, 1955; Melville Dalton, *Men Who Manage.* New York: John Wiley & Sons, 1959.

tions from the existing evidence for it. That evidence is certainly not conclusive, but it is provocative. I will confine myself to the field I know best: the management of human resources within the industrial enterprise. It will be clear, I believe, that there are broader implications.

Two Fundamental Propositions

Underlying the argument are two self-evident but widely ignored propositions:

I. *Behind every attempt to influence others lies a theory* (or a belief or a conviction) *concerning cause and effect in human behavior.* In the absence of a theory of some kind—explicit or implicit, conscious or unconscious—there would be no basis for choice among the many actions one could take in order to exert influence. Purely random behavior would occur. It is obvious, since random behavior is not what occurs (after infancy, at least), that there exists some form of theory about what cause will lead to what effect.

I do not speak here of theory in the scientific sense of a systematic, integrated, research-based hypothesis. Nevertheless, I do refer to hypothesis—the guess, the generalization, the belief—about what will happen if one takes a certain course of action. Every individual holds many such theories, and they are not necessarily consistent, integrated, or conscious. Nevertheless, they underlie every action he takes for the purpose of controlling or influencing the behavior of others.

Our theories come primarily from three sources. First, they come from the folklore of our culture: spare the rod and spoil the child; money talks; man is a competitive animal.

Second, they come from personal experience and observation. Out of our individual experience we develop many generalizations and beliefs about cause and effect, which we use as the occasion requires. One man says, "People respond to praise and recognition"; another says, "You must let people learn from making mistakes"; another says, "People are fundamentally dishonest." The attempts of each of us to influence others are guided by our own personal theories.

The third source of theory is scientific knowledge. Such knowledge is also based on observation and experience, but it has been obtained under a particular set of rules concerning the gathering of evidence and exposed to certain tests of validity. Such knowledge is therefore more consistent internally and more trustworthy than folklore or individual beliefs. It is less subject to the influence of error and bias.

More important, however, scientific knowledge includes hypotheses that we would never arrive at through *direct* observation and experience. This is not generally true of the other sources of theory. We do not experience the earth as round, nor observe directly the behavior of microbes, nor perceive objects as systems of energy particles whirling in space. We perceive light directly, but not infrared radiation. The fact of the existence of infrared radiation can be demonstrated, but not directly through our senses.

One of the consequences of this characteristic of scientific knowledge is that we are sometimes slow to accept it. The widespread rejection for long periods of the Copernican theory of heliocentricity, Harvey's theory of the circulation of the blood, Pasteur's "germ theory" of disease, Freud's theory of unconscious mental processes was in part due simply to the fact that these theories were not consistent with the direct observation of everyday life and experience. This presents a formidable obstacle when the theory concerns the nature of man and his behavior, and I will return to it.

Our attempts to influence others reflect all three of these sources in varying degrees, but the central point is that every such attempt we make—whether in the casual interactions of everyday life, or in setting a rule or a policy, or in planning an elaborate strategy of change—is a direct consequence of our theories. Were this not so, we could not choose how to act in order to influence others.

II. *The effectiveness of any attempt to influence or control behavior is a function of the adequacy of the theory of cause and effect behind it.* To be sure, other factors have a bearing on the outcome of attempts to influence. One's skill may be inadequate; the theory may be correct but the situation wrongly perceived. Nevertheless, the more correct and complete the theory, the higher the probability that attempts to influence will be successful. Consider a theory of cause and effect that propose that man responds to logic and reason *alone*. (Incidentally, many attempts to control behavior are based implicitly on exactly this theory.) An extreme example of another kind is the paranoid whose world is peopled entirely with enemies. The inadequacy of his theory clearly affects the success of his efforts to influence. In fact, his theory is so inadequate that he may have to be institutionalized to prevent him from acting in accord with it.

The Prevailing Theory: Cause-Effect Equals Stimulus-Response

Everyday experience and the folklore that is a distillation of such experience produce quite naturally a common theme with respect to man's conceptions of cause and effect in human behavior. It is that behavior is a direct function of rewards and punishments, or the expectation of them. Thus, although there are a great many variations on the theme, the prevailing theory of cause and effect is a simple stimulus-response theory. It has to do with what forms of reward and punishment (actual or promised) lead to what behavior.

Tactical choices are affected by many other considerations, such as the intelligence of those whom we attempt to influence, their attitudes, values, personality traits, social and economic status, and so forth. Nevertheless, the primary causal relationship underlying our attempts to control or induce change in behavior is almost universally conceived in simple stimulus-response terms, with rewards and punishments as the stimuli. Until relatively recently, much scientific theory was in accord with this interpretation of everyday observation and experience.

The practices of industrial management in its attempts to influence behavior reflect this theory of cause and effect. A central concern is expressed in the question: how can we motivate people to contribute to the objectives of the enterprise? Management's answers are expressed in terms of one of three strategies of control. Each is based on a stimulus-response theory of cause and effect. One—"hard" management—relies heavily on the threat of punishment. One—"soft" management (relatively out of favor today, but prominent a few years ago)—relies primarily on the promise of reward. The third, and the most common currently, is a compromise between the other two: "firm-but-fair" management.

The tactics employed with all three of these strategies are strikingly similar (because they are all based on the same fundamental conception of cause and effect). There *are* differences in the way procedures are administered. However, organization structure, wage and salary administration plans, incentive plans, suggestion plans, safety programs, promotion policies, and a considerable number of control procedures (e.g., budgets and accounting controls based on indices of performance such as profitability, costs, quality) are almost universal methods for influencing or controlling human effort in the service of organizational objectives.[2] These become the basis for control through rewards and punishments administered by management, with differing emphasis, depending on which of the three strategies is the accepted one. The staff department responsible for developing many of the control procedures in one large company states its view thus: "Measure every possible aspect of performance and use the measures as needles." Other companies attempt similarly to measure performance, but some use the measurements differently to control behavior.

Cause and Effect in the Physical World

I should like now to trace certain historical similarities and differences in our ability to control human behavior, on the one hand, and physical phenomena, on the other, and to relate these to theories of cause and effect. My central point is that the tremendous growth in man's ability to control physical phenomena since the late nineteenth century is a consequence of a change in conceptions of cause and effect in the natural sciences, which began about then to have an impact. A parallel change in theories of cause and effect has been taking place more recently in the behavioral sciences, and the way is now open for a similar accelerated "technological" growth in our ability to control human behavior.

[2] A thoroughgoing research-based analysis of the consequences of managerial strategies on behavior is presented in Rensis Likert, *New Patterns of Management*. New York: McGraw-Hill Book Company, 1961.

There are some important barriers in the path, however, and I will also touch on them.

From the time of Aristotle until the late nineteenth century—a period of 24 centuries—cause and effect in the physical world was conceived in terms of the direct application of force to object, a theory similar to the stimulus-response theory now prevalent with respect to human behavior. Aristotle conceived of an "unmoved mover of the planets"; Galileo (1600 A.D.) conceived of force as producing *change* in physical movement; Newton brilliantly developed and elaborated a set of laws—his *Principia*—in terms of the same underlying conception of cause and effect.

This virtually universal theory had genuine utility. It permitted the development of a variety of methods of control (cf. Proposition I above). The printing press, the steam engine, and textile weaving equipment are typical illustrations. Inventions based on direct observation and experience, probably reinvented many times and carried on through cultural folklore (e.g., the wheel, the lever, the paddle, and the water wheel), were of course of much earlier origin. They are also consistent with the Aristotelian theory of cause and effect.

However, technological developments like those that have occurred during the present century had to await extensions well beyond this simple force-on-object theory. Methods of control of physical phenomena such as television, radar, the production of synthetic materials, the relay, the transistor, and the maser could not even be conceived until the development of what is now referred to as "general systems theory." This conception of cause and effect is so powerful, so much more adequate than early conceptions, that it has enabled us to multiply our ability to control physical phenomena manyfold in a mere half century.

The differences between this new conception of cause and effect and the earlier one are many, and they lead to some of the profound intricacies of modern theoretical physics.[3] However, certain aspects of systems theory are readily understandable, and examples of technological advances resting on them abound in our everyday life. A few of these will serve to indicate the profound significance of the shift that has occurred.

Technological Consequences of Systems Theory

First, physical phenomena of all kinds are conceived today in terms of energy. Objects, from the atom to the universe, are complex patterns of energy, structural and functional systems of interrelated and interacting variables. Cause and effect relationships within and between systems occur in many ways. Some of these are produced by direct force on object, in a manner consistent with Aristotle's theory. Some involve highly indirect relationships, as, for example, when a change in one part of a system has indirect consequences elsewhere in the system. Rachel Carson in *Silent Spring* is talking in system terms when she traces biological and social consequences of the use of certain chemicals to control insects.

A tiny release of energy within a system can trigger large effects (the relay). A small input of energy to a system can be magnified millions of times (amplification). A large input of energy can produce minute changes within the system (X-ray therapy). Energy can be changed from one form to another (television, radio).

By changing the structure of systems, products can be produced having almost any desired characteristics (syn-

[3] Mary B. Hesse, *Forces and Fields*. New York: Philosophical Library, 1962.

thetics). Catalytic agents, themselves inert (i.e., exerting no force on object), can substantially alter the structure and behavioral characteristics of systems (ceramics, metals). Corning Glass Company recently announced a new, almost shatterproof glass. The process of manufacture is similar to that of many other glass products; the difference lies in the addition of a single ingredient to the conventional raw materials.

Modifications of variables in the environment of a biological system (e.g., the concentration of salt in sea water in which a certain fish embryo is developing) can produce major changes in the structure of the organism (a single eye rather than one on each side of the head). Tissue (a particular organ) transplanted into an embryo at a certain stage of development maintains its original properties (as an "extra" organ); at other stages it is completely absorbed into the embryonic system.

These are a few relatively simple examples from an almost limitless array of currently known ways of influencing or controlling physical phenomena. Some could be directly based on a mechanical (i.e., Aristotelian) conception of cause and effect. A great many, however, could only be imagined (and thus chosen) as methods of control in the light of modern systems theory.

Some Behavioral Research with Systems Implications

Systems conceptions of cause and effect are not new in the behavioral sciences. Psychological conceptions of personality, of the process of human development, of socialization, of perceptual and intellectual processes, have been strongly influenced by systems theory during the past quarter century. Modern cultural anthropology reflects a systems orientation. Gestalt psychology, which was a direct attempt to relate physical and psychological phenomena in systems terms, has been influential since the thirties. Modern sociological theory is heavily systems oriented. The transition in behavioral science began later than it did in the physical sciences, but it has been accelerating in recent decades.[4]

Let us examine two or three among many lines of research in the behavioral sciences which reflect a systems point of view and which carry implications for control within the field of industrial management. First, consider a few aspects of human behavior in face-to-face groups.

Face-to-Face Groups and Leadership

Typical current managerial views about groups are summed up in the comment that a camel is a horse put together by a committee. Groups are widely believed by laymen to be inherently inefficient and time-wasting. They are said to be incapable of making decisions and particularly of implementing them. They are asserted to be poor problem-solving mechanisms in comparison to individuals. They tend, it is believed, to create conformity pressures, which reduce the individual number to the level of the least common denominator. All these are widely believed to be inherent properties of groups, modifiable only within narrow limits.[5]

Unfortunately, we cannot get along without groups. As a result, much time and effort is devoted to attempts to influence and control them, even within the narrow possibilities commonly believed to exist. The prevailing common-

[4] An excellent overview of developments within the field of psychology can be obtained from *Contemporary Psychology: A Journal of Reviews*, published by The American Psychological Association, Washington, D.C.
[5] William H. Whyte, Jr., *The Organization Man*. New York: Simon & Schuster, 1956.

sense theory underlying these attempts is the mechanical Aristotelian one: cause and effect consists in the direct application of force to (human) objects. If group effectiveness can be improved at all, it will be through the qualities and skills of the leader. Group behavior, in other words, is almost completely a function of the rewards and punishments given to or withheld from the group by the leader.

The body of research evidence amassed during the past two-and-a-half decades about group behavior indicates that the behavior of the leader is indeed a factor affecting performance. But it also indicates clearly and unequivocally that group effectiveness is a function of many intricate relationships (among properties of the group as a system) which the leader can control, if at all, only indirectly. Group behavior is a function of a large number of interacting variables of which leadership, conceived in Aristotelian terms, is but one.[6]

Table 1 lists a few of the more important of these variables. It does not indicate what is known today about some of the interrelationships among them. Take the three variables, leadership skills, open communications, and climate, for example. Effective problem solving depends obviously upon the availability of all relevant data. Among the relevant data for group problem solving are the ideas, reactions, and feelings of group members with respect to the issue under discussion. Typically, many of these are not expressed in the group (although sometimes in informal discussion elsewhere) and are therefore not available to influence the decision. Nevertheless, the failure to make them available often

[6] Robert Tannenbaum, Irving Weschler, and Fred Massarik, *Leadership and Organization: A Behavioral Science Approach*. New York: McGraw-Hill Book Company, 1961; Bernard Bass, *Leadership, Psychology, and Organizational Behavior*. New York: Harper and Brothers, 1960.

seriously impairs the implementation of the decision. More importantly, if they were available, these data could frequently be used by the group in ways that would lead to a better, sometimes to an appreciably more innovative, solution to the problem.

TABLE 1　Some Variables Influencing the Effectiveness of Face-to-Face Groups

The Nature of the Task	Methods of Decision Making
Commitment to the Task	Methods of Managing Conflict
"Openness" of Communications	Flexibility of Structure
Skills of the Formal Leader	The "Climate"
Member Skills	Group Standards and Norms
Power and Status Differences	Attention to Group Maintenance
Cohesiveness of the Group	The Use of Performance Data

Genuinely "open" communications cannot be obtained either by threats of punishment or promises of reward on the part of the leader. They are possible only within a climate of mutual trust and respect. Such a climate is a function of the relationships among the members, as well as between the leader and the members. It is a complex, delicate property of the group system, and it is altered by many subtle influences, only a few of which can be controlled by direct manipulation of rewards and punishments.

There are ways of influencing the development of such a climate and thus of improving substantially the effectiveness of a group. They are not methods that would be chosen —or even imagined—by leaders who think in mechanical rather than in systems terms. In fact, such leaders are characteristically unaware of the existence of many phenomena within their groups that influence importantly the quality of group effort. They view the poor performance, the mediocre problem-solving competence, as inherent properties of groups, and as a result they never discover the potential power of a genuinely effective team.

A considerable body of scientific knowledge exists concerning cause-and-effect relationships among the variables that make up the group system.[7] It can have almost no "technological" impact, however, so long as the prevailing theory is that group behavior is simply a function of leadership conceived in Aristotelian terms. Meanwhile, accepted methods of control, based on that prevailing theory, produce exactly the characteristics of groups that are the source of our pessimistic views about them!

Intergroup Phenomena

A similar situation obtains in the interaction between group systems. Friction and antagonism between functional groups in organizations, behavior that is severely detrimental to the achievement of organizational goals, these are not the inevitable result of "human nature" or (as is so often assumed) of the personalities of particular individuals.[8] However, it cannot be controlled by the conventional, relatively primitive tactics of leadership any more than the behavior of a vehicle in space can be controlled by the application of the principle of the lever or the water wheel.

Methods analogous to those employed in laboratory courses in physical science, designed to create an awareness

[7] Dorwin Cartwright and Alvin Zander (Eds.), *Group Dynamics: Research and Theory.* Evanston, Ill.: Row, Peterson, 1962 (2nd ed.).

[8] Robert R. Blake and Jane S. Mouton, *Group Dynamics: Key to Decision Making.* Houston, Texas: Gulf Publishing Co., 1961, especially Chap. 6, "The Story Behind Intergroup Conflict"; Paul R. Lawrence, et al., *Organizational Behavior and Administration.* Homewood, Ill.: Irwin-Dorsey, 1961; Dalton, *op. cit.*

of the nature and consequences of those kinds of intra- and intergroup phenomena that are not apparent at the level of common-sense observation and experience, are being employed increasingly today to help improve managerial competence in controlling group behavior. This educational "technology," stimulated by behavioral scientists in a number of academic institutions who are associated with the National Training Laboratories (a division of the National Educational Association) in Washington, D.C., is developing at an accelerated pace, and it is having an impact on practice and theory not only in industry, but in government, religious institutions, education, and many other organizations.[9] The power of this technology of training lies in the fact that it derives from systems theories of group behavior and leadership.

The Organization of Work

A second line of research concerns the organization of work. Again there exists a substantial amount of research-based knowledge in this area. I will report some of the findings of one group of behavioral scientists who are on the staff of The Tavistock Institute of Human Relations in London. They have been interested for a decade in what they call "socio-technical systems," namely, in systems consisting of a social organization around a technological process. Certain of their findings stemmed from observa-

[9] Warren G. Bennis, Kenneth D. Benne, and Robert Chin (Eds.), *The Planning of Change*. New York: Holt, Rinehart and Winston, 1961, especially Parts 3 and 4; Chris Argyris, *Interpersonal Competence and Organizational Effectiveness*. Homewood, Ill.: Irwin-Dorsey, 1962; Robert R. Blake and Jane S. Mouton, *The Induction of Change in Organizations*. Scientific Methods, Inc., Austin, Texas.

tion of work structures in semiautomated coal mines in England.[10]

Table 2 shows the differences between two forms of or-

TABLE 2   Contrasting Socio-Technical Systems
in British Coal Mines *

	Conventional	Composite
Number of men in three-shift operation	41	41
Number of segregated task groups	14	1
Individual job variation:		
task groups worked with	1	5.5
tasks worked	1	3.6
shifts worked	2	2.9
Quality control exercised by	separate inspectors	the group itself
Pay system	individual incentives	group payment for total task performance
Work organization determined by	management and staff experts	the men themselves

* Same technology, same coalseam.
Adapted from Trist, *op. cit.*

ganization that they observed. The "conventional" system was developed according to standard industrial-engineering practice. The work was divided into small, routine, repeti-

10 Eric L. Trist, *Socio-Technical Systems.* Tavistock Institute of Human Relations, London, England, April 1960; Eric L. Trist and K. W. Bamforth, "Some Social and Psychological Consequences of the Longwall Method of Coal Getting." *Human Relations*, 1951, *4*, No. 1. (A book covering the whole series of research studies in this field is currently under preparation by Dr. Trist.)

tive tasks, each performed continuously by an individual who was rewarded under an incentive plan for his own effort. Each man worked, either alone or in a small subgroup, on his assigned task. When breakdowns occurred, the men waited while help was brought in to repair the equipment. At shift changes, the outgoing crew simply stopped work, leaving any necessary cleanup for the next shift. Quality control was maintained by independent inspectors.

The "composite" system had been developed largely by the men themselves, and important phases of it were administered by them. The pay system was in terms of the total performance of a team of 41 men working a rotating three-shift schedule with the semiautomated equipment in one area of the mine. Each man worked on a variety of tasks and with several subgroups, depending upon his skills and the requirements of the situation. When difficulties or breakdowns occurred, the team restructured itself to deal with them. The quality control was in the hands of the team rather than being administered by outside inspectors. The men themselves selected the team and determined work assignments, including shift rotation.

Table 3 indicates some of the differences in performance between the two forms of organization. One among several interesting comparisons concerns absenteeism. Under the conventional system there were the usual attempts to reduce absenteeism and to improve the safety of performance (based on mechanical conceptions of force on human object). However, probably because the composite system created a much higher security in an inherently dangerous situation, as a result of the interdependence and mutual help within the team, absenteeism from all causes, *including accidents*, was cut to less than half the rate that obtained under the conventional system. Not force on object, but a restructuring of the socio-technical system produced these results. This is particularly interesting when one thinks of the money, manpower, and effort normally expended on safety campaigns, and how necessary is a regular "shot in the arm" to keep the accident rate from slipping upward. Similar implications are apparent in the differences between other forms of managerial control under these two work systems.

TABLE 3   Contrasting Results from Differing Socio-Technical Systems in British Coal Mines *

	Conventional	Composite
Productivity index	78	95
Hours per man per shift required for cleanup from previous shift	1.32	0.03
Additional (outside) help required per shift—percentage of total force	6	0
Percentage of shifts with interruptions of the equipment cycle	69	5
Absenteeism—percentage of possible shifts:		
without reason	4.3	0.4
sickness or other	8.9	4.6
accidents	6.8	3.2
	20.0	8.2

* Same technology, same coalseam.
  Adapted from Trist, *op. cit.*

One additional note on this Tavistock research: the theory developed from it was transplanted to another culture (India) and another industry (cotton textiles), and an experiment was conducted there to change a conventional system to a composite one. The results, maintained over several years, were as predicted from the coal-mining stud-ies.[11]

I have chosen to cite the Tavistock study, not because it stands alone, but because it makes its point rather directly and simply. Many other significant studies, here and abroad, are cited in the references throughout this paper.

Controlling the Motivation to Work

As a final example see Figure 1. These data summarize the findings of a study conducted by Herzberg and his col-leagues in engineering and accounting departments in fifteen manufacturing plants in the Midwest United States.[12] The findings cast new light on an old problem: the relationship between satisfaction and productivity. Up to a decade and a half ago, there was a belief—and some evidence to support it—that these two variables were positively correlated. More recent evidence, as well as direct experience, indicated that the correlation was zero. As Rensis Likert and his colleagues have shown, data can be obtained indicating almost every possible relationship between these variables.

The direct contribution of the Herzberg study is to recast the problem and thereby reveal some significant character-istics of the relationship between these two variables. In-directly, this study has profound implications for managerial strategy.

The factors labeled "dissatisfiers" operate to produce *both* low performance and negative attitudes *when they are not equitably administered*. However, when employees feel they

[11] A. K. Rice, *Productivity and Social Organization: The Ahmedabad Experiment*. London: Tavistock Publications, 1958.
[12] Frederick Herzberg, Bernard Mausner, and Barbara Bloch Snyder-man, *The Motivation to Work*. New York: John Wiley & Sons, 1959 (2nd ed.).

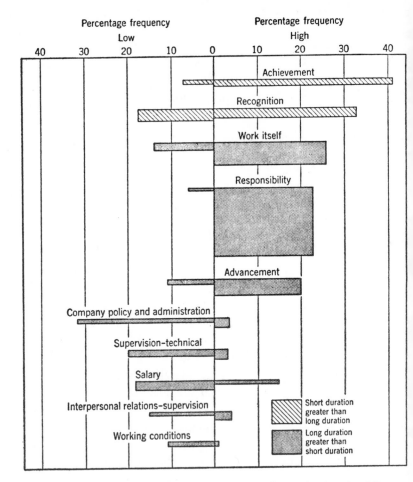

Fig. 1 Comparison of "dissatisfiers" and "satisfiers." The length of line represents the frequency of occurrence; the thickness of line represents the duration of effects. From Herzberg, Mausner, and Snyderman, *op. cit.*, p. 81, reproduced with permission of John Wiley & Sons, New York.

are fairly rewarded with respect to these variables, increasing the rewards further has only a modest effect on either satisfaction or performance. The suggestion is that these "extrinsic" (controlled from without the individual) rewards are highly important, but primarily in a negative sense. What they will produce as motivators is essentially a fair day's work for a fair day's pay (along with negative side effects if they are not equitably administered), and not much more. To be sure, the relationships are not perfect, as the chart indicates. The trends, however, are clear and substantial.

The "dissatisfiers" include the primary stimuli on which management typically relies to "motivate people." They are the obvious methods of control if the theory of cause and effect is one of force on object, or of externally and directly manipulated rewards and punishments.

The "satisfiers," on the other hand, are associated with high satisfaction, high motivation, high performance. The "work itself" variable refers to the way the job is structured. Does it offer the individual opportunity to use his training, his skill, his talents? Or does it limit him, force him to operate below his level of competence? (Cf. Tavistock findings.) "Advancement" refers not only to promotion but to opportunities to grow and develop on the present job.

The significant point about most of the satisfiers (recognition and promotion are exceptions) is that the rewards and punishments associated with them are "intrinsic." They are obtained by the individual as a direct result of his own effort; they are inherent in the activity. It is not possible to provide an individual with a sense of achievement, or with the satisfaction associated with the acceptance of responsibility, by controlling extrinsic rewards and punishments. If the conditions in the system consisting of the individual in his work environment are appropriate, he will seek this satisfaction through his own efforts. If the conditions are inappropriate, he is prevented from doing so. *The methods of control related to most of the satisfiers are not conceivable within the framework of an Aristotelian theory of cause and effect.*

The Herzberg study was conducted with "socio-technical systems" in which the technology is essentially intellectual rather than mechanical, and the personnel are professional rather than manual workers. Generalizations drawn from it must take account of these and other characteristics of the system. They do, however, offer important leads with respect to the perennial managerial question: "How do you motivate people?"

An answer which is fully consistent both with these findings, and with what is now known about the human being in systems terms, is that significant "intrinsic" motivations are *properties of the human system.* The human being is not a passive machine requiring extrinsic force to induce motion; he is an organic system. Many powerful forms of motivated behavior can be *released* by appropriate manipulations of environmental variables. However, such possibilities will only be perceived as a result of a shift from an Aristotelian to a systems conception of cause and effect. The situation is comparable in some ways to that of the potentialities for control of disease opened up by Fleming's work with penicillin.

Does Increased Control Threaten Human Freedom?

The Herzberg study also contains some interesting implications for the question of whether improvements in our ability to control behavior as a result of increased scientific knowledge will lead to situations such as are implied by Huxley's *Brave New World* or Orwell's *1984*. The tacit assumption of both these writers, and of many who are concerned about the social consequences of improved methods of control, is one that equates control with constraint. This is natural if one thinks of cause and effect in simple stimulus-response terms. Even rewards are constraining if they are controlled and allocated by others (because they can then also be withheld).

However, if we think of control in terms of adaptation to natural law—if we define it as taking actions that yield predicted consequences—the Herzberg findings carry other implications. The significant modifications that they reported in system variables, associated with high motivation, high performance, and high satisfaction, involved the removal of constraining forces, such as unduly close supervision and work organization, which prevented the individual from utilizing his capabilities and training. We know from other studies that these variables, when controlled so as to produce constraint, tend to create resentment, either apathy or rebellion, and low performance.[13]

Adaptation to natural law in this case, then, involves both the equitable administration of extrinsic rewards which are associated with "low-level" physiological and security needs, and freeing the individual from constraints that prevent him from obtaining the intrinsic rewards associated with "high-level" ego and self-actualization needs.[14]

The broader implication is that, as economic development

[13] See Likert, *op. cit.*, Chaps. 2–4. Likert also cites some research (see Chap. 7) that explains the Herzberg finding that "recognition" operates either as a satisfier or dissatisfier.

[14] Abraham H. Maslow, *Motivation and Personality*. New York: Harper, 1954; Douglas McGregor, *The Human Side of Enterprise*. New York: McGraw-Hill Book Company, 1960, Part I.

and the development of physical technology increasingly free mankind from the basic struggle for physical survival, control by means of constraint will be less and less effective, and control by *removing* constraints upon intrinsic rewards will become correspondingly more effective. The apparent paradox—that control thus becomes absence of control, or abdication of leadership, or anarchy—disappears if we recognize that the removal of constraint involves the manipulation of a variety of system variables. Similarly, in controlling physical phenomena, the shift from a force-on-object to a systems approach involves manipulation of *different* variables, not elimination of control. The "predictable results" will not occur as a result of inaction, but only as a result of highly sophisticated actions based on knowledge of the relationship among system variables. But in this case these actions give human beings more freedom, not less!

Obstacles in the Path

The behavioral sciences are still in an early stage of development, it is true, but the body of existing knowledge is considerably larger than most people recognize, *and it is having only a limited influence on practice.* However, the reasons for this state of affairs are not the commonly stated ones. The problems are not to any major extent due to lack of communication, or to esoteric scientific terminology, or to inability to find practical ways to apply research findings, or to any of the half-dozen other frequent criticisms by managers of behavioral scientists, and vice versa. These are casual factors, to be sure, but they are minor compared to others that are more basic. The development of a new technology associated with the control of human behavior will remain slow until these more basic difficulties are confronted and overcome. Let us turn to an examination of some of them.

Ambivalence about Control of Behavior

One problem has already been alluded to. It concerns a deep and common ambivalence about the whole question of control of human behavior. On the one hand, managers and politicians and advertisers and teachers and labor leaders and parents and a host of others are aware that increased ability to influence behavior would help them to achieve their goals (whether these be selfish or altruistic, exploitative or humanitarian). On the other hand, we are also all aware that increased knowledge in this field would subject each of us to greater control *by others*, and we suspect that such control would often interfere with our achievement of our own goals. Thus we face a dilemma that is not easy to resolve, although the implications of studies like that of Herzberg et al., discussed above, point to a possible resolution.

Historically, it is significant how steadfastly and powerfully man has clung to the belief that he is outside the natural order. Any scientific discovery that has threatened his centrality, his superiority, his uniqueness in nature, has been rejected, sometimes for surprisingly long periods. For example, the work of Copernicus, Kepler, and Galileo on our astronomical system—which showed that the earth, and therefore man, is not at its center—was completed around 1600. It was not until two centuries later (in 1822) that the Catholic Church officially accepted these findings. In more recent times, one thinks of the work of Darwin or Freud, and of the response, not only of the public at large, but of many of their fellow scientists as well.

The scientific belief that man is a part of the natural order

—the faith that his behavior is largely, if not wholly, lawful and therefore potentially predictable—cuts squarely across some deep-seated and long-standing human values. Man's image of himself, his anxieties over being manipulated, his very identity, are profoundly challenged whenever these values are held to be in question. If the contention with which I began this paper is even partly true, it represents just such a challenge.

Our ambivalence about control is a form of conflict, and it is true of all conflict, whether within individuals or between them, that any attempts to deal with it by suppression or avoidance have negative consequences, sometimes very serious ones. The only way to minimize these consequences is to bring the issue into the open, examine it fully, and seek a genuine resolution. This process of "working through" conflicts is difficult and sometimes painful. In some cases there appears to be no complete resolution; however, compromising, or living with a conflict that has been genuinely confronted and accepted as inevitable, produces fewer negative side effects than suppressing it or pretending that it is not there. In many cases, the confrontation results in an innovative answer that eliminates the conflict or reduces it substantially.

A number of things become clear if we are willing to confront the conflict raised by the issue of control of human behavior. One is the demonstrable fact that, to a very substantial degree, the behavior of man *is* governed by law (and is therefore potentially controllable). However, an additional fact is that control always involves adaptation to natural law, not bending it to our will. It is fascinating—and remarkably comforting too—to discover that some of the most powerful ways to control human behavior require *reduction* or *removal* of forces that are preventing man from realizing his own potentialities, rather than the strengthening of forces that either drive or constrain him.

Unlike the earlier naïve theory that the simple substitution of reward for punishment (soft versus hard management) or the abdication of leadership, would yield more effective behavior, systems theory clearly indicates the necessity for modifying certain kinds of variables rather than others. A human group, for example, does not become an effective problem-solving team as a result of the abdication of the leader. The necessary modifications in the system include the development of commitment to the group task, self-control exerted by the members in the interests of the task, a supportive climate, and certain methods for managing conflict and making decisions.

The development of these characteristics of the system reduces the necessity for the conventional (force-on-object) controls exerted by the leader and makes possible the effective use of group resources. In addition, such changes free each member to realize his own potentialities to a greater extent, and this provides significant intrinsic rewards.

More effective group behavior rests, then, on the reduction or removal of the kinds of control that many people characteristically fear and resent, and the substitution of controls that open up new opportunities for all members to achieve their goals. External control and self-control are to some degree reciprocal. Effective group behavior rests also in part on an appropriate balance between intrinsic rewards and extrinsic ones. This, too, means control that is *less* constraining.

This is only one example of the way in which our natural ambivalence toward the matter of control of human behavior may be *reduced* by confronting the conflict. The more we learn about human behavior through behavioral science research, the more it becomes clear that many exploitative methods of control are inconsistent with natural law, and that they are often essentially self-defeating because of the side effects they generate. Too little knowledge is indeed a dangerous thing!

I would not minimize the possibilities for unscrupulous or damaging use of methods of control that may accompany the growth of scientific knowledge in this field.[15] Knowledge is itself neutral with respect to human values; it can be used for good or for evil. We have had ample evidence of this in modern technology. But, as is the case with the development of nuclear physics, the possibilities for the use of new scientific knowledge to improve human welfare are also present. And here, at the "technological" level, is where man can make choices that are unavailable to him in the absence of that knowledge. Shall we limit ourselves to primitive methods for helping mankind solve the problems that beset us, because we fear the responsibility for choice that knowledge brings?

What is Reality?

The second problem we face when we attempt to use the knowledge gained from behavioral science is the frequently expressed criticism that much of this knowledge is unrealistic and impractical. This is a way of saying that it is not consistent with everyday experience and observation, a phenomenon I alluded to earlier in discussing the sources of our theories about cause and effect.

The same problem exists in the physical field. Direct experience and observation often conflict with scientific

15 Loren Baritz, *The Servants of Power*. Middletown, Conn.: Wesleyan University Press, 1960.

knowledge. We tend to reject the latter, sometimes violently, when it challenges deep-seated beliefs about ourselves. The rejection is usually less violent and shorter lived, however, when the truth of scientific theory is demonstrable in fairly obvious ways. Columbus sailed to the "West Indies" without falling off the edge of the earth, Pasteur's dogs went mad when he injected them with rabies, Fulton's steamboat traveled independently of the wind, and the Wright brothers' aeroplane flew.

But if the demonstration is not conclusive, and particularly if we have a strong ego investment in another theory, the stage is set for decades of resistance. Darwin and Freud encountered the real force of this phenomenon. It is an important factor in delaying the technological developments that could today improve our ability to control behavior.

The manager who has developed a strategy of control on the basis of his own experience and the folklore consistent with it, and who has discovered that it works, tends quite naturally to be somewhat incredulous when it is suggested that a very different strategy, based on assumptions that are inconsistent with his experience, would work better. If, in addition, the "scientific" theory contradicts deep-seated and largely unconscious assumptions built into his adjustment and his ways of coping with the world, his skepticism will turn readily into outright rejection.

Some field experiments concerned with managerial strategy in industrial organizations have suffered this fate. Valid and reliable data, which were threatening to management, have been flatly rejected, the experiments terminated, and behavioral science branded as useless or even dangerous.

It has so far been difficult to provide management with convincing demonstrations that strategies of control based on a systems theory of cause and effect are more effective than those based on an Aristotelian theory. As in any attempt at an innovative technological development, a substantial amount of trial-and-error experimentation is inevitable. This takes time and risk capital, both of which require initial faith in the outcome. As indicated above, the strategies indicated by systems theory sound bizarre precisely because the theory is not consistent with much everyday experience. Terms like "idealistic," "soft-headed," "impractical," suggest the degree of faith that exists currently.

Also, conventional strategies of control have built into existing industrial organizations a host of tactical procedures on which management depends for assurance that things are going all right, or that corrections can be made before serious damage is done (to the annual profit-and-loss statement especially). Many of these procedures would necessarily be drastically modified, or held in abeyance, during an experiment, thus producing uncertainty and anxiety "upstairs." Since the necessary period of time for an experimental development and test of a new strategy is a matter of years, not weeks or months, it is a rare management indeed that will undertake the risks involved.

There are, of course, many limited and small-scale research and development projects that are helping to build slowly a body of evidence supporting the systems approach. However, these tend to be more convincing to the behavioral scientist than to managers. They can often be "explained away" without too much difficulty. (A favorite device for this purpose is to dismiss such research results as representing merely a "Hawthorne effect.")

One substantial effort to produce a convincing demonstration has been so close to failure several times during the five years since it began that only the courage and commitment of a few highly influential members of top management have kept it going. Even their faith, however, could not prevent major adjustments and modifications of the experiment to meet the pressures of "reality." The ultimate results will be positive, but the initial conception of developing and testing a genuinely innovative managerial strategy consistent with systems theory has to a considerable extent gone by the board in the face of these pressures. It will be easy for the skeptic to conclude that this experiment "proves" that the theory behind it is unrealistic and impractical.

The Need for Simplicity and Order

The growth of science has led to a gradual appreciation of the immense complexity of natural phenomena. Scientists on the frontiers of any field of knowledge continually face a baffling array of conflicting and virtually incomprehensible phenomena. Even a firm faith in the underlying orderliness of nature is regularly challenged. Moreover, as order does emerge, it generally proves to be far from simple. The scientist must learn to live in muddy water. He confronts ambiguity, uncertainty, and complexity most of the time.[16]

On the other hand, man feels a deep necessity to find simplicity and order in his world so that he can have some basis for emotional security, for prediction, and for action. Unless we human beings can discover order and predictability in the everyday world, we do not know how to behave so that we can survive and achieve our goals.

The ubiquity of this need is evident in the cosmologies of every society in recorded history. Man's natural way of

[16] Some of the research on creativity suggests that it is associated with the ability to live without discomfort in such "muddy waters." See Donald W. MacKinnon, "The Nature and Nurture of Creative Talent." *The American Psychologist*, 1962, *17*, 484–495.

dealing with this problem is a function of certain properties of his nervous system. He is able not only to perceive differences and similarities, but to perceive *selectively*, ignoring many aspects of the buzzing confusion with which he is surrounded and attending to others. This process is reinforced by his desires and his fears to a degree that sometimes makes him quite unable to perceive or to understand more than he "wants" to.

The processes are far more complex than these words suggest, but they enable us to *impose* order on the world.[17] We abstract, we generalize, we perceive regularity and predictability whether it is there in fact or not. Many of our attitudes, our habitual ways of responding, even some of our most central personality characteristics represent particular ways of imposing order on the confused and disorderly array of events and phenomena that confront us daily. Acute anxiety often results when we cannot thus reduce complexity to simplicity.

These characteristics of the human system are clearly assets, but they can also be liabilities. Much of the time, the order we impose on nature (physical and human) enables us to live effectively and in reasonable comfort, even when that order is unrealistic from a scientific point of view. For our practical purposes as laymen, we get along with explanations and ideas about cause and effect that are grossly different and far simpler than those derived from scientific research. It is ordinarily of little or no consequence, for example, that we view matter as solid, whereas the scientific conception is one of systems of energy particles whirling in

[17] Gordon W. Allport, *Personality and Social Encounter*. Boston: Beacon Press, 1960; O. J. Harvey, David E. Hunt, and Harold M. Schroder, *Conceptual Systems and Personality Organization*. New York: John Wiley & Sons, 1961.

space. *However, we cannot design a space vehicle or create a new synthetic product on the basis of our layman's point of view.*

Sometimes, of course, the order we impose on the world is so grossly incorrect or oversimplified that many of our fellow laymen (let alone scientists) perceive it to be unrealistic. In the political sphere, the John Birch Society is an illustration. Here the underlying anxiety in the face of complexity is transparent.

The Manager's Needs for Simplicity and Order

The reduction of managerial strategies of control to the three alternatives of hard, soft, or firm-but-fair represents another way of imposing an oversimplified order on a complex set of phenomena. In one sense it is a helpful process. It enables the manager to make decisions and take actions in an environment that will not stand still while he makes a scientific analysis of the enormously complex system in which he is embedded, that will not wait while he experiments with changes in a wide array of variables to see what works best.

It is not surprising, therefore, that the world of organized human effort as the behavioral scientist sees it often becomes a source of anxiety for the manager. Is the latter not perhaps correct in insisting that he must have a simple "order," a set of principles to follow, an easily understood and practical strategy, even if it is far from ideal? After all, he can point to the obvious fact that the traditional strategies work. Industrial organizations achieve their objectives in a fairly satisfactory way. (But so do the horse-drawn plow and the steam locomotive!)

As for the strategies of technological development in

the physical field, the manager can get along reasonably well with the layman's self-imposed and oversimplified perception of reality (unless he is directly administering a research-and-development activity). He can hire scientists and engineers to face the complexities of nature and to choose the strategies for innovation. He can make the business decisions about investment in the activity and the utility of the products and processes yielded by it without ever facing the necessity for understanding or accepting the scientific view of reality.

Not so for managerial strategies of control of human behavior. The significant current products of research and development in this field simply cannot be used successfully by the manager unless he understands and accepts the underlying scientific view of reality with respect to cause and effect in human behavior. In this field he is not the scientist, but he is the engineer. If he persists in imposing an order on reality that reduces it to the level of common sense, he will be in the same position as a man attempting to design a modern weapons system without knowledge of the physical sciences, or a man attempting to practice medicine without knowledge of modern biology and chemistry.

The assertion is often made that management is becoming a profession. If so, one of the central skills of the professional in any field is his use of scientific knowledge to solve practical problems. The role of the manager today is one that requires professional competence for effective performance. As far as managing human resources are concerned, Aristotelian conceptions of cause and effect are incompatible with professional competence.

The compensation for becoming more professional is an increased ability to influence and control. In the simple world of Aristotle, there were, inevitably, few ways to control nature (e.g., the lever and the water wheel). If the manager's world today is similarly oversimplified, his strategies of control are likewise limited. As he becomes more professional—more able to utilize scientific knowledge in solving practical problems—his power to control increases manyfold. However, this is often difficult for him to perceive, because he can gain this power only by abandoning certain firmly established habits and beliefs, for example, that his power consists solely in the direct application of force to human object.

It is not surprising that many managers seek and find ways out of this dilemma. They reject the findings of the behavioral sciences, or they give them lip service without utilizing them in action, or they misinterpret them in ways that yield simple panaceas or "principles" of action consistent with their existing beliefs and their needs.

Why We Fail to Exploit Behavioral Science

If there is power inherent in existing behavioral science knowledge—and the evidence clearly suggests there is—we face some difficult problems in making it real rather than potential. I have outlined some "restraining forces" among many that hold the system at its present slow rate of change. If the change is to be accelerated, it would seem that ways must be found: (1) to gain acceptance of the idea that at least large areas of human behavior are fundamentally subject to law, (2) to help managers shift from Aristotelian concepts of cause and effect to the systems concepts characteristic of modern science, (3) to obtain acceptance of the fact that reality in human behavior, as elsewhere in nature, is not always as it appears to direct observation and experience, and (4) to persuade managers to face the complexity of the phenomena of human behavior in organized settings and, as a result, to modify the grossly oversimplified order that they have understandably imposed on the world.

As a corollary, managers must also be somehow persuaded that the search for the "one best way" of managing human resources is not only futile but irrelevant, that attempting to choose between hard, soft, and firm-but-fair strategies is like choosing between various lengths of levers for the purpose of putting a space vehicle on the moon. These are not, in fact, separate strategies, but tactics within a single strategy: the manipulation of extrinsic rewards and punishments in order to control behavior.

The obstacles to the conversion of knowledge into power that we have examined are not primarily rational, even though the consequences of removing them would be changed ways of perceiving and thinking. They include deep and powerful emotional factors associated with man's convictions about his own nature, with his central values, with his tried and tested perceptions of the human world and his convictions concerning appropriate modes of coping with it. They are the foundation of whatever confidence he has acquired in his ability to act and respond to others in ways that enable him to survive and prosper. They have strongly influenced the nature of the conceptual "glasses" he has fashioned to enable him to impose meaning and order on a world that might otherwise be frighteningly complex and unpredictable.

Obviously, rational argument and intellectual persuasion are frail tools for the purposes of changing these emotional forces. They may gain a precarious lip service, but they do not touch the real obstacles. Confronting management with "facts," research findings, and behavioral science theory often amounts to little more than applying force to human object, thus increasing tension in the system and producing self-defeating side effects or outright rejection.

Overcoming these obstacles, then, is a more complex and difficult task than management usually suspects when it decides "to utilize behavioral science knowledge," for example, by instructing the personnel staff to familiarize itself with the field in order to determine what it has to offer, or by hiring a behavioral science consultant, or even by adding a new behavioral science department to the organization.[18]

I have indicated why I believe that the contention I began with is correct, and why the rate of development of a more effective "human technology" is slow. The issue is not *whether* such a technology will be developed, but rather *how fast?* My impression is that the current rate of development is generally slower than it might be. It is substantially slower in some fields than in industry, although the need— from the point of view of society at large—may be greater. I have tried to indicate that the fundamental problems are similar across many fields of human concern even though their scope and complexity may differ substantially.

The fundamental point is an old one. Knowledge is power. However, it is only potential power. Perhaps we are today a bit too tentative in confronting our very natural ambivalence toward turning knowledge into power. However, such a confrontation can only have salutary consequences. Health, whether in the individual, the group, the organization, or the society, is never achieved by ignoring or suppressing underlying conflicts, but by discovering how to manage them. This we can choose to do.

[18] There are many things that behavioral scientists have been doing successfully in industry without encountering in any serious way the obstacles I have been describing. Work in selection, some kinds of training, and attitude measurement represents obvious illustrations. However, research and development, because they touch on the manager's way of managing human resources, confront these obstacles immediately.

Bibliography of Douglas McGregor

The Sensitivity of the Eye to the Saturation of Colors. Ph.D. thesis, Harvard University (Psychology), Cambridge, Mass., 1935; Abstract in *Journal of Experimental Psychology*, 1936, *19*, No. 5.

Scientific Measurement and Psychology. *Psychological Review*, 1935, *42*, 246–266.

Should There Be Academic Prerequisites for Graduate Work in Psychology? *Psychological Bulletin*, 1937, *34*, 501–509.

The Major Determinants of the Prediction of Social Events. *Journal of Abnormal and Social Psychology*, 1938, *33*, 179–204.

A Study of Public Opinion Among a Group of Industrial Workers. *Psychological Bulletin*, 1938, *35*, 650–651.

The Attitudes of Workers toward Layoff Policy. *Journal of Abnormal and Social Psychology*, 1939, *34*, 179–199.

Motives as a Tool of Market Research. *Harvard Business Review*, 1940, *19*, No. 1, 42–51.

The Genesis of Attitudes toward Management (with Conrad M. Arensberg). *Psychological Bulletin*, 1940, *37*, 433–434.

Industrial Relations and National Defense: A Challenge to Management (with Irving Knickerbocker). *Personnel*, 1941, *18*, No. 1, 49–63.

Determination of Morale in an Industrial Company (with Conrad M. Arensberg). *Applied Anthropology*, 1942, *1*, No. 2, 12–34.

Union-Management Cooperation: A Psychological Analysis (with Irving Knickerbocker). *Personnel*, 1942, *19*, No. 3, 520–539.

Conditions of Effective Leadership in the Industrial Organization. *Journal of Consulting Psychology*, 1944, *8*, 55–63; *Advanced Management*, 1944, *9*, No. 4, 148–153; and in S. D. Hoslett (Ed.), *Human Factors in Management*. New York: Harper and Brothers, 1951, pp. 23–35.

The Foreman's Responsibilities in the Industrial Organization. *Personnel*, 1946, *22*, No. 5, 296–304.

The Nature and Use of Authority. In University of Michigan, Bureau of Industrial Relations *Addresses on Industrial Relations*, 1946, pp. 85–87.

Re-evaluation of Training for Management Skills. In *Training for Management Skills*. New York: American Management Association, Personnel Series, No. 104, 1946.

Foreword, The Consultant Role and Organizational Leadership: Improving Human Relations in Industry. *Journal of Social Issues*, 1948, *4*, No. 3, 2–4.

The Staff Function in Human Relations. *Journal of Social Issues*, 1948, *4*, No. 3, 5–22.

The Supervisor's Job (18 pages, mimeo). Address before Management Forum of E. I. du Pont de Nemours & Company, Wilmington, Delaware, April 16, 1948.

The Dewey and Almy Chemical Company: A Case Study (with Joseph N. Scanlon). Case Studies in Causes of Industrial Peace under Collective Bargaining, No. 3. Washington, D.C.: National Planning Association, 1948, 88 pp.

Toward a Theory of Organized Human Effort in Industry. In *Psychology of Labor-Management Relations, Proceedings of the Meeting*. Champaign, Ill.: Industrial Relations Research Association, 1949, pp. 111–122.

Changing Patterns in Human Relations. In National Industrial Conference Board, *Conference Board Management Record*, 1950, *12*, No. 9, 322, 323; and in M. deV. Richards and W. A. Nielander (Eds.), *Readings in Management*. Cincinnati, Ohio: South-Western Publishing Company, 1958.

How Can We Go Forward? Panel discussion on The Untapped Potential in Labor-Management Relations. In *Mobilizing America's Strength for World Security*. Report of 19th Annual New York Herald-Tribune Forum, October 23–25, 1950. New York: Herald Tribune, Inc., 1950, pp. 65–68.

Line Management's Responsibility for Human Relations. In *Building Up the Supervisor's Job*. New York: American Management Association, Manufacturing Series No. 213, 1953, pp. 27–35.

The Changing Role of Management. *The Technology Review*, 1955, *57*, No. 6, 287–290; and in H. C. Thole and C. C. Gibbons (Eds.), *Business Action in a Changing World*. Chicago: Public Administration Service, 1956, pp. 9–16.

The Human Side of Enterprise. In *Adventure in Thought and Action*, Proceedings of the Fifth Anniversary Convocation of the M.I.T. School of Industrial Management, June 1957, pp. 23–30; also (in condensed form) in *The Management Review*, 1957, *46*, No. 11, 22–28.

An Uneasy Look at Performance Appraisal. *Harvard Business Review*, 1957, *35*, No. 3, 89–94.

The Significance of Scanlon's Contribution. Chapter 2 in Frederick G. Lesieur (Ed.), *The Scanlon Plan: A Frontier in Labor-Management Cooperation*. New York: The Technology Press and John Wiley & Sons, 1958, pp. 7–15 (fifth printing by The M.I.T. Press, Cambridge, Mass., 1964).

The Scanlon Plan through a Psychologist's Eyes. Chapter 8 in Frederick G. Lesieur (Ed.), *The Scanlon Plan: A Frontier in Labor-Management Cooperation*. New York: The Technology Press and John Wiley & Sons, 1958, pp. 89–99 (fifth printing by The M.I.T. Press, Cambridge, Mass., 1964).

Management Development: The Hope and the Reality. In *Proceedings of the American Petroleum Institute*, Section III, Division of Refining, Addresses and Reports. New York, May 28, 1959, pp. 272–277.

The Human Side of Enterprise. New York: McGraw-Hill Book Company, 1960.

The Role of Staff in Modern Industry. Chapter 1 of Part III in George P. Shultz and Thomas L. Whisler (Eds.), *Management Organization and the Computer.* Glencoe, Ill.: The Free Press, 1960.

New Concepts of Management. *The Technology Review*, 1961, *63*, No. 4, 25–27; and in *The Executive*, 1961, *4*, No. 12, 13–15.

Behavioral Science—What's In It For Management? National Industrial Conference Board, *Business Management Record*, 1963, *25*, 32–44.

Can You Measure Executive Performance? *International Management*, 1964, *19*, No. 6, 59–61.

Index

THE M.I.T. PRESS PAPERBACK SERIES